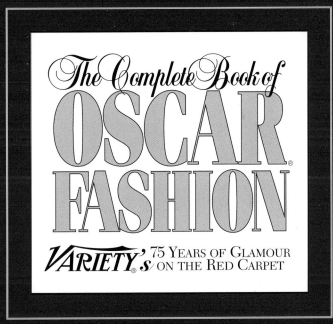

The Complete Book of OSCAR FASHION

VARIETY's 75 Years of Glamour on the Red Carpet

The Complete Book of OSCAR® FASHION

Variety's 75 Years of Glamour on the Red Carpet

REEVE CHACE

Reed
PRESS

An EYE book

EYE

Copyright © 2003 EYE Quarto, Inc.

Conceived, designed and produced by
EYE
276 Fifth Avenue
Suite 205
New York, NY 10001

Editor: Michael Driscoll
Cover Design: Sheila Hart
Interior Design: Rowan Moore/doublemranch.com
Proofreader: Edwin Kiester Jr.
Indexer: Kitty Chibnik

Publisher: William Kiester

First published in North America by
Reed Press
360 Park Avenue South
New York, NY 10010

Manufactured in China.

ISBN 1-59429-001-6

Library of Congress Cataloging-in-Publication data requested.

g f e d c b a

Many thanks go to my friend and publisher, William Kiester, who conceived of and brought this book to fruition through his guidance and clever suggestions. He was truly a collaborator. Thanks also go to my editor, Michael Driscoll, who pulled all the pieces together under crushing deadlines, and with the many exigencies placed upon him by his return to New York. I must also thank the folks over at Photofest and Jorge Jaramillo at The Associated Press for their assistance in the research of photos for this book, and Rowan Moore for her wonderful design and coolness under pressure. And finally, thanks to my friends and family for their patience and support during the writing of this book.

CONTENTS

FASHION PREVIEW

TAKE A WALK DOWN THE RED CARPET
AND THROUGH THE HISTORY OF OSCAR FASHION

For 75 years the Academy Awards have celebrated the magic of film. Each year, the top actors and actresses in Hollywood have donned their finest duds to prepare for their appearance on the red carpet. What started out as a small, private ceremony is now one of the biggest events of the year in Hollywood, covered by media outlets around the world. The Oscars give celebrities the chance to show their true colors, to step out of their various roles of the previous year and put on costumes of their own choosing. Some have chosen wisely, securing their status as the beautiful, serious actors they wish to be. Others have taken missteps on the red carpet that have haunted them throughout their careers. Whatever they wear, we onlookers are fascinated by how our screen idols choose to present themselves when it's time to let their real personalities shine through.

From glamorous getups to outrageous mistakes to sartorial risks that paid off, the following pages present the pageantry of Oscar fashion in photographs culled from 75 years of Academy Awards ceremonies. The photos put it all on display, leaving nothing to the imagination and sparing no one a repeat performance of his or her worst fashion decision. From Joan Crawford to Joan Allen, Katharine Hepburn to Cate Blanchett, the history of fashion at the Oscars is all here, in a no-holds-barred exhibit of how Hollywood has presented its best face to the world. Here is a preview of the characters you can expect to find ...

THE ELEGANT ORIGINAL

The original elegance of old Hollywood can be found in **Norma Shearer's** 1930 floor-length gown with mink-trimmed sleeves.

THE DEMURE DARLING

Luise Rainer made modesty a virtue in 1937 in her bloused gown with a high neck and long, full sleeves.

THE CLASSIC BEAUTY

Classic Hollywood beauties **Ingrid Bergman** and **Jennifer Jones** showed off the good looks and styling of the war years in their 1945 arrival at the awards.

THE CHIC INGÉNUE
Audrey Hepburn defined the new look of chic in her lacy tea-length gown of 1954.

THE GLAMOUR GIRL
Natalie Wood and **Warren Beatty** epitomized the glamour of old Hollywood as they swept into the awards in 1962.

THE DARING BLONDE
Inger Stevens raised eyebrows as well as hemlines when she wore this mini-dress to the Oscars in the fashion-forward 60s.

THE BOHEMIAN
Ali McGraw's crocheted cap was emblematic of the era of hippies and free love.

THE SOPHISTICATE

Uma Thurman made Oscar fashion history when she wore this elegant Prada gown to the 1995 awards. The dress is seen by many as inspiring a return to style and grace after years of more ostentatious dressing.

THE *1920s* AND *1930s*

A GRAND TRADITION COMMENCES

When the first Academy Awards show was staged, in May of 1929, the Roaring Twenties were still in full swing. The flapper look was all the rage, and young women reveled in their ability to wear loose-fitting, comfortable evening clothes that left them free enough to dance the night away. But the party was silenced with the stock market crash of October 1929 and the Great Depression that followed. Public revelry was no longer in vogue, and evening wear took on a more restrained look of elegance. Floor-skimming silk or satin gowns cut on the bias were the most popular looks for big nights out. By going against the natural weave of the fabric, the bias cut allowed the dress material to flow naturally around women's figures, bringing an emphasis on womanly curves back into fashion. Hollywood, of course, showed off the most glamorous of these looks: actresses were still prevented from showing too much cleavage on film, so gowns with very low-cut backs became popular, allowing actresses to show some skin while skirting the censorship issue. Naturally, as film became a more accessible and increasingly popular pastime with the public, the look of Hollywood elegance filtered down to the masses. Soon no elegant woman would be seen out after dark without her satin or silk gown and fox-fur stole.

FASHION ON FILM

It Happened One Night (1934)

In this film still from It Happened One Night, *Claudette Colbert's runaway heiress shows off a beautiful example of the most popular silhouette for evening: a floor–skimming, slim–fitting, bias–cut silk gown that exudes elegance.*

The Women (1939)

Adrian designed the costumes for this film, which starred only women and featured a plot that revolved around acquiring clothes. As a result, there was plenty of fashion inspiration to be found, and the costumes were modeled by some of the most popular actresses of the day: Joan Crawford, Norma Shearer, Rosalind Russell and Joan Fontaine.

DESIGNERS TO THE STARS: 1920s and 30s

ADRIAN (1903-1959)

The Original Designer to the Stars

In the days when studio costume designers were akin to today's top couture designers, what Hollywood actresses wore on film could influence entire generations of women. And so it was with legendary studio designer Gilbert Adrian, who made the careers of some of the best-known women in film history. Adrian designed the costumes for hundreds of films, including *Camille*, *The Wizard of Oz* and *The Philadelphia Story*, and dressed Jean Harlow, Greta Garbo, Joan Crawford and Norma Shearer, both onscreen and off.

EDITH HEAD (1903-1981)

Head of the Class

Edith Head became the head designer at Paramount in 1938, and spent most of her illustrious career there before branching out to design for MGM, Columbia and other studios. Head caused a sensation with the costumes she designed for Mae West in *She Done Him Wrong*, a film that broke box-office records thanks in part to Head's sexy designs. During her prolific career, Head designed the costumes for over 500 films, won eight Academy Awards, and was nominated for an Oscar 33 times. She has dressed innumerable stars, including Elizabeth Taylor, Grace Kelly, Barbara Stanwyk and Audrey Hepburn.

ELSA SCHIAPARELLI (1890-1973)

Shocking Elsa

Elsa Schiaparelli designed shockingly innovative yet wearable clothes. She was influenced by American sportswear, but always added her own twist, whether in the form of elaborate embroidery or by using buttons molded in the shape of bugs and sugar cubes. Her inventive looks attracted the attention of well-known artists, many of whom she collaborated with on her designs, like Salvador Dali, Pablo Picasso and Man Ray. Her signature color was a brilliant pink, and after naming a trademark lipstick and perfume Shocking, she has gone down in the annals of fashion history as Shocking Elsa. Katharine Hepburn, Greta Garbo and Joan Crawford were just some of the many actresses who wore her designs.

*19*29   THE VERY FIRST CEREMONY

1ST
ACADEMY AWARDS
May 16, 1929
Blossom Room
Hollywood Roosevelt Hotel
HOSTS:
DOUGLAS FAIRBANKS
WILLIAM C.
deMILLE

In the beginning, the Oscars were a small affair that felt more like a private party than the massive public spectacle they are today. The winners were announced months ahead of time, few photos were taken, and the whole ceremony lasted just minutes. In fact, no one really knows what that year's Best Actress winner, Janet Gaynor, even wore to the ceremony. There was little coverage in the press, and, more than anything, the Oscars existed to unite Hollywood insiders and promote public goodwill toward the rapidly growing film industry.

AND THE OSCAR® GOES TO...

Best Production:
Wings

Best Artistic Quality of Production:
Sunrise

Best Direction (Drama):
Frank Borzage,
Seventh Heaven

Best Direction, (Comedy):
Lewis Milestone,
Two Arabian Knights

Best Actress:
Janet Gaynor,
Seventh Heaven,
Street Angel and *Sunrise*

Best Actor:
Emil Jannings,
The Last Command and
The Way of All Flesh

FIRST LADY OF FILM

This publicity still shows the first Best Actress Oscar winner in history, **Janet Gaynor**, who didn't even talk in the three films for which she was honored. The first Oscar ceremony conferred awards on films from both 1927 and 1928.

©A.M.P.A.S.®

NOT SO QUIET ANYMORE 1930

The awards ceremony was held twice in 1930: once in the spring, at what has become the traditional time to stage the Oscars, and again that year in November, in order to catch up with honoring all the new "talking pictures" that had flooded movie theaters that year. Befitting the new state of the film industry, this was also the year the Awards were first broadcast over the radio. Despite the fact that the broadcasts could only be heard, not seen, the stars dressed as if the world was watching.

SHEAR ELEGANCE
MGM's costume designer Gilbert Adrian created the gown that **Norma Shearer** wore to the November 5 ceremony of 1930; it was the same gown she wore in *The Divorcee*, the very film for which she was honored. Slim-fitting and cut on the bias, the gown draped elegantly around her slender frame. Mink-trimmed sleeves added just the right touch of Hollywood glamour, as did her diamond bracelets.

©A.M.P.A.S.®

2ND
ACADEMY AWARDS
April 3, 1930
Cocoanut Grove
Ambassador Hotel
Los Angeles
HOST:
WILLIAM C. deMILLE
ACADEMY PRESIDENT

AND THE 1928-29 OSCAR® GOES TO...

Best Picture:
The Broadway Melody

Best Director:
Frank Lloyd, *The Divine Lady*

Best Actress:
Mary Pickford, *Coquette*

Best Actor:
Warner Baxter, *In Old Arizona*

3RD
ACADEMY AWARDS
November 5, 1930
Fiesta Room
Ambassador Hotel
Los Angeles
HOST:
CONRAD NAGEL

AND THE 1929-30 OSCAR® GOES TO...

Best Picture:
All Quiet on the Western Front

Best Director:
Lewis Milestone,
All Quiet on the Western Front

Best Actress:
Norma Shearer, *The Divorcee*

Best Actor:
George Arliss, *Disraeli*

1931

THE BIG SLEEP

4TH
ACADEMY AWARDS
November 10, 1931
Sala D'Oro, Biltmore Hotel
Los Angeles
HOST:
LAWRENCE GRANT

The 1931 ceremony was graced by then-U.S. Vice President Charles Curtis, but his presidential presence lacked punch. So many important Hollywood figures got up to speak that the awards themselves weren't doled out until after midnight, resulting in a tedious, drawn-out show. The ban on liquor may have caused spirits to flag, but even in the throes of the Depression, the stars managed to shine.

AND THE OSCAR® GOES TO...

Best Picture:
Cimarron

Best Director:
Norman Taurog,
Skippy

Best Actress
Marie Dressler,
Min and Bill

Best Actor:
Lionel Barrymore,
A Free Soul

©A.M.P.A.S.®

HOLLYWOOD ROYALTY
Two of Hollywood's best-loved actors, **Marie Dressler** and **Lionel Barrymore**, accepted Oscars for their performances as Best Actress and Best Actor, respectively. Dressler wears an ermine coat over her black lace dress, while Barrymore looks dapper in a traditional tux with white bow tie.

TIES NOT OPTIONAL 1932

The awards show in 1932 seemed a rather ho-hum affair—until a last-minute count of the votes revealed a tie between Best Actor nominees Fredric March and Wallace Beery. The eleventh-hour announcement would prove to be the last bit of Oscar excitement until the next awards show, which wouldn't be held until almost a year and a half later.

5TH
ACADEMY AWARDS
November 18, 1932
Fiesta Room, Ambassador Hotel
Los Angeles
HOST: CONRAD NAGEL,
ACADEMY PRESIDENT

©A.M.P.A.S.®

AND THE OSCAR® GOES TO...

Best Picture:
Grand Hotel

Best Director:
Frank Borzage,
Bad Girl

Best Actress:
Helen Hayes,
The Sin of Madelon Claudet

Best Actor (TIE):
Fredric March,
Dr. Jekyll and Mr. Hyde;
Wallace Beery,
The Champ

Honorary Award:
Walt Disney
for the creation of
Mickey Mouse

TIE BREAKER
Co-Best Actor-winner **Fredric March** and wife **Florence Eldridge** sit at a table at the Academy Awards. Her close-cropped, curled hair and off-the-shoulder gown are more characteristic of the 1920s than the 30s.

1934

FRANK'S MISTAKE

6TH
ACADEMY AWARDS
March 16, 1934
Fiesta Room, Ambassador Hotel
Los Angeles
HOST: WILL ROGERS

No one needed a drink more than Frank Capra after his embarrassing gaffe at the first ceremony to serve alcohol since Prohibition was lifted. Capra thought he had won the Oscar for Best Director, thanks to host Will Rogers' omission of the winner's last name. But after making it halfway to the stage, Capra sheepishly returned to his seat after realizing that the real winner was *Cavalcade* director Frank Lloyd. Less embarrassed was Diana Wynyard, who glowed in a satin gown that producers hoped would come to define what they envisioned as Hollywood's most glamorous event. Unfortunately, photographs of the 1934 event are rare.

AND THE OSCAR® GOES TO...

Best Picture:
Cavalcade

Best Director:
Frank Lloyd,
Cavalcade

Best Actress:
Katharine Hepburn,
Morning Glory

Best Actor:
Charles Laughton,
The Private Life of Henry VIII

WILL THE RIGHT FRANK PLEASE STAND UP?

Frank Capra in 1935, the year he really did win the Oscar for Best Director, for *It Happened One Night*.

©A.M.P.A.S.®

A CLOSE CALL 1935

The biggest crowd yet turned out for the 1935 awards show, but some prominent faces were missing: all the Best Actress nominees except Bette Davis. After a write-in campaign put Davis on the nomination ballot, the other Best Actress nominees were so sure she was going to win that none of them bothered to attend the ceremony. After the surprising upset was announced, winner Claudette Colbert was called to the Biltmore Bowl just before boarding a train for New York. She was at the ceremony for all of six minutes, but without a doubt made one of the greatest entrances and exits in Oscar history.

7TH
ACADEMY AWARDS
February 27, 1935
Biltmore Bowl, Biltmore Hotel
Los Angeles
HOST: IRVIN COBB

AND THE OSCAR® GOES TO...

Best Picture:
It Happened One Night

Best Director:
Frank Capra,
It Happened One Night

Best Actress:
Claudette Colbert,
It Happened One Night

Best Actor:
Clark Gable,
It Happened One Night

©A.M.P.A.S.®

TRAVELING IN STYLE
Claudette Colbert accepts her award for Best Actress from **Shirley Temple** in a suit designed for traveling—not expecting to win, she was on her way to New York for a vacation when her victory was announced. Her enormous corsage softens the practical look of the suit, as does her fur coat, curled hair and cleverly tilted cap.

SPOTLIGHT
on Gowns: 1930

EXQUISITE TASTE

Mary Pickford picked a winner for the April 3, 1930, ceremony with this silk chiffon bias-cut dress, a beautiful example of the style of the times. Intricate beadwork at the waist yoke and an enormous diamond brooch at the bustline added dazzle to this exquisite gown. But a gown like this doesn't just appear without advance planning: so confident was she of her nomination, Pickford sent for her dress in Paris before the selections were even announced.

In the first year of the 30s, styles from the 20s were a holdover: *Closely cropped, curled hair and multiple strands of pearls* were still fashionable.

A softly draped bow was affixed to the bodice by a *sparkling diamond brooch.*

A *closely fitted bodice* exemplified the new silhouette of the 30s—the loose, bloused look of flapper dresses quickly became a thing of the past.

Sparkling bands of diamonds added glitter at the wrists and picked up the shine of the beading on the gown.

A *delicately beaded hip* yoke helps define the slimmer, more elegant silhouette of evening wear.

A *bias-cut skirt* allows the fabric to flow in gentle waves down to just above the toes.

BETTE'S REVENGE 1936

A boycott against the Academy by members of the directors, actors and writers guilds made for a small number of famous faces in the crowd at the eighth Academy Awards show. But one very famous face did stand out, framed by a simple frock: Bette Davis, still feeling robbed of the Best Actress Oscar the previous year, showed up in a plain printed dress more suited for a picnic than the biggest night in Hollywood. It was an obvious rebuff to the Academy members who had snubbed her the year before. Whether she deserved it or not, she was chastised roundly by both the press and the Academy.

8TH
ACADEMY AWARDS
March 5, 1936
Biltmore Bowl, Biltmore Hotel
Los Angeles
HOST: FRANK CAPRA

©A.M.P.A.S.®

MOHR MAKES THE CUT

Best Cinematographer-winner **Hal Mohr** was at home listening to the radio when a friend called to tell him he had won. He shaved, threw on a tux, and made it to the show in time to pick up his Oscar. **Evelyn Wanable** presented in a gorgeous two-toned gown embellished with art deco brooches at the neckline and waist sash.

©A.M.P.A.S.®

AND THE OSCAR® GOES TO...

Best Picture:
Mutiny on the Bounty

Best Director:
John Ford,
The Informer

Best Actress:
Bette Davis,
Dangerous

Best Actor:
Victor McLaglen,
The Informer

UNDERSTATED IS AN UNDERSTATEMENT

Bette Davis quite deliberately put little care into her choice of a simple (and not particularly flattering) cotton dress with wide lapels. As a result, she looks more like the help than a movie star standing next to Best Actor-winner **Victor McLaglen**, who dressed more appropriately for the occasion.

*19*37 THE CROWDS RETURN

Glamour returned to the Academy Awards in 1937, with stars filing into the sold-out theater en masse to sip champagne and be seen in their finest duds—all except for Best Actress-winner Luise Rainer, who was summoned from home to the ceremony by a studio publicist who had heard she was scheduled to win the Oscar. She threw on the only dress she had handy.

9TH
ACADEMY AWARDS
March 4, 1937
Biltmore Bowl, Biltmore Hotel
Los Angeles
HOST: GEORGE JESSEL

AND THE OSCAR® GOES TO...

Best Picture:
The Great Ziegfeld

Best Director:
Frank Capra,
Mr. Deeds Goes to Town

Best Actress:
Luise Rainer,
The Great Ziegfeld

Best Actor:
Paul Muni,
The Story of Louis Pasteur

Best Supporting Actress:
Gale Sondergaard,
Anthony Adverse

Best Supporting Actor:
Walter Brennan,
Come and Get It

SLIPPED IN

Luise Rainer was at home in her slippers when an MGM publicist called to tell her to come down to the awards show to accept her Oscar. She dutifully made up her face and dashed out the door in the only dress she had on hand, a rather plain crepe gown with long, bloused sleeves—hardly the glamorous creation studio heads wanted their actresses to be seen wearing.

©A.M.P.A.S.®

RAINER DELAY 1938

The 1938 Oscars had to be delayed for a week due to record flooding in Los Angeles, and by the time the rescheduled show was up and running, few stars bothered to show up and collect their Oscars. Greta Garbo, Spencer Tracy and even the host George Jessel bowed out, leaving the producers with a show that had little star wattage to make it shine. Luise Rainer—who was once again called at home and told she had an Oscar waiting to be picked up—made one of the few star appearances, with an unmade face and a dress she kept covered under a fur coat.

10TH
ACADEMY AWARDS
March 10, 1938
Biltmore Bowl, Biltmore Hotel
Los Angeles
HOST: BOB BURNS

©A.M.P.A.S.®

AND THE OSCAR® GOES TO...

Best Picture:
The Life of Emile Zola

Best Director:
Leo McCarey,
The Awful Truth

Best Actress:
Luise Rainer,
The Good Earth

Best Actor:
Spencer Tracy,
Captains Courageous

Best Supporting Actress:
Alice Brady,
In Old Chicago

Best Supporting Actor:
Joseph Schildkraut,
The Life of Emile Zola

DEJÁ LU

For the second year in a row, **Luise Rainer** proved the most photogenic star of the evening, this time in a white fur coat that she quickly threw on to accept her Oscar for Best Actress in *The Good Earth*.

FINAL TAKE

The last awards show of the decade proved to be yet another tepid one in terms of star attendance and public interest. Ticket sales were down, and the prettiest star of the evening was the young Shirley Temple. But one screen legend managed to make up for years past—Bette Davis, who won the Best Actress Oscar for her role in *Jezebel*, turned heads in her show-stopping gown.

11TH
ACADEMY AWARDS
February 23, 1939
Biltmore Bowl, Biltmore Hotel
Los Angeles
HOST: FRANK CAPRA

AND THE OSCAR® GOES TO...

Best Picture:
You Can't Take It With You

Best Director:
Frank Capra,
You Can't Take It With You

Best Actress:
Bette Davis,
Jezebel

Best Actor:
Spencer Tracy,
Boys Town

Best Supporting Actress:
Fay Bainter,
Jezebel

Best Supporting Actor:
Walter Brennan,
Kentucky

BETTE-ING ON WINNING

Bette Davis glided into the awards like a swan on a still lake in this glamorous Colette gown adorned with egret feathers that swept up dramatically around her neck and shoulders. The full-skirted gown was an extravagant fashion statement in a decade when the slim silhouette was much more favored.

STRANGE DOS

The gowns get all the attention, but plenty of stars have arrived at the Oscars with hair or hats that have demanded a share of the spotlight. Though most actresses opt for demure French twists, chic chignons, or sexy blowouts, some women prefer to don scene-stealing headgear on Oscar night. Here we present a panoply of hairdos, hats and wraps that were a cut above the rest.

RUFFLED FEATHERS

The two-foot-high rooster-feather headdress **Cher** wore in 1986 was the talk of the town—and the tabloids—for years to come.

BABS' BOB

Barbra Streisand's outlandish 1969 Oscar outfit needed an equally awkward hairdo, and she got it with this teased and layered bob that somehow went perfectly with her clownish getup.

HAUTE HIPPIE

Linda Lovelace, star of the adult film *Deep Throat*, looked lovely in 1974 in a white lace sunhat that gave her a fresh-from-the-country look—hardly what fans had come to expect from her, or from Hollywood's most glamorous evening.

CAPPED OFF

Because her head had been shaved for her role as Queen Elizabeth I in *The Virgin Queen* (1955), **Bette Davis** covered it up for her 1955 appearance at the Oscars with a jeweled and sequined gold helmet with a peaked crown.

DOWN IN FRONT!

Erykah Badu gave a nod to traditional African culture with her giant head wrap at the 2000 Oscars—but whoever sat behind her was probably not the happiest Oscar attendee.

THE 1940s

THE (FASHION) SHOW MUST GO ON

World War II changed the course of history, and its chilling effects could be felt even in Hollywood. As the 1940s got underway, the elegant and sumptuous styles of the 30s gave way to more practical and modest fashions. Wartime rationing was partly responsible for the subdued new look, as a shortage of dressmaking materials meant that designers had to make clothes that were necessarily slimmer and more snug. Hats were among the few things that could express a woman's individuality, as milliners still had enough material available to create the fantastical headgear that helped offset the more severe style of dressing that characterized the era. Even so, during the years of heaviest fighting, the Academy asked stars to tone down their most glamorous getups out of respect for the gravity of world events. While several Hollywood actresses acquiesced to the request, many others decided they would give the public what they figured it really wanted: pure, unbridled Hollywood glamour. Thankfully, the war was soon over, and as the 40s unfolded, fashion at the Oscars became something new entirely. Led by Christian Dior's revolutionary "new look" of 1947, designers returned to more generous cuts in their skirts and gowns. Luxury was back, and the stars began to dress in a manner that heralded the return to unabashed glamour.

FASHION ON FILM

Casablanca (1942)

Ingrid Bergman wears the uniform of well-dressed women in the 40s: a slim dress that shows off a trim waist, a hemline that falls just below the knee, an eye-catching, elegant hat and the finishing touch, gloves.

The Philadelphia Story (1940)

The aristocratic Katharine Hepburn was an obvious choice to play a spoiled heiress in this film costarring James Stewart. She wears a glamorous gown designed by costume designer Adrian.

DESIGNERS TO THE STARS: 1940s

CRISTÓBAL BALENCIAGA (1895-1972)
The Serious Spaniard

Balenciaga was born the son of a tailor in the Basque region of Spain. His dramatic clothes were influenced by the dark passion of Spain's flamenco dancers, toreadors and artists, and most often came in dusky shades of brown and black. He was noted for creating evening gowns with complicated details like capes, trains and flounces, and he designed the first pillbox hat. Fittingly, seriously sexy stars like Marlene Dietrich and Ingrid Bergman were some of his most faithful customers.

JACQUES FATH (1912-1954)
A Flair for Fetching Frocks

A Parisian who started out designing hats, Jacques Fath soon turned to creating beautiful clothes that clamored for attention. He didn't bother to sketch out his designs first, but rather draped fabric directly onto his models. His talent for creating clothes with a spirit of extravagance turned him into the darling of Hollywood. Rita Hayworth was his most important client; he designed the wedding dress for her marriage to prince Aly Khan. His career was cut short when he died of leukemia at 42.

PIERRE BALMAIN (1914-1982)
Architectural Details

Pierre Balmain left architecture school to study dressmaking. The careful construction that would have served him well as an architect translated to a talent for crafting exquisite gowns that were both elegant and romantic. He also designed many of the costumes for Hollywood films in the 40s and 50s. He created the dress Brigitte Bardot wore in *And God Created Woman*, an outfit and a role that were enormously influential in securing her sex-symbol status.

1940

SWEPT AWAY

The stars put on their finest ermine and pearls for this year's ceremony. They knew they were being filmed for a documentary on the ceremonies, and studios had implored their stars to dress with all the star power they could muster. Notably, the brightest luminary of the night, Best Actress-winner Vivien Leigh, was one of the most casually attired in her relatively plain dress.

12TH
ACADEMY AWARDS
February 29, 1940
The Cocoanut Grove
Ambassador Hotel
Los Angeles
HOST: Bob Hope

AND THE OSCAR® GOES TO...

Best Picture:
Gone With the Wind

Best Director:
Victor Fleming,
Gone With the Wind

Best Actress:
Vivien Leigh,
Gone With the Wind

Best Actor:
Robert Donat,
Goodbye, Mr. Chips

Best Supporting Actress:
Hattie McDaniel,
Gone With the Wind

Best Supporting Actor:
Thomas Mitchell,
Stagecoach

©A.M.P.A.S.®

FRANKLY, SHE DIDN'T GIVE A DAMN

Vivien Leigh was probably the only woman to wear a print dress to the Academy Awards in 1940. Her dress (decidedly not a gown) looks more like a sundress than eveningwear, but the floral print and full skirt stood out among the flashier, sleeker gowns that filled the ballroom that evening. The Best Actress-winner's one nod to Oscar-night dazzle is the huge, clear gem low in her décolletage.

NOT IN KANSAS ANYMORE

An eye-catching brooch keeps **Judy Garland's** rabbit-fur coat together as she clutches her mini-Oscar and gets kissed by Mickey Rooney. Long white gloves and a decorative bloom add flourish to the fur coat, and give the young star a touch of grown-up glamour.

©A.M.P.A.S.®

PATRIOT GAMES 1941

The specter of war had begun to dim the bright lights of Hollywood—President Roosevelt even spoke by telephone at the awards to pay tribute to Tinseltown's patriotism. But full-blown restraint hadn't yet overtaken the stars' style of dressing for the awards, and many chose daring costumes for the evening's events.

13TH
ACADEMY AWARDS
February 27, 1941
Biltmore Bowl
Biltmore Hotel
Los Angeles
HOST:
WALTER WANGER
ACADEMY PRESIDENT

PUFFED-UP WITH PRIDE

In balloon sleeves and a deeply cut neckline, **Lynn Fontanne** (right) may be fore-shadowing the styles of *1001 Arabian Nights*. This was a very unusual look for the time, but Fontanne pulled it off gracefully.

AND THE OSCAR® GOES TO...

Best Picture:
Rebecca

Best Director:
John Ford,
The Grapes of Wrath

Best Actress:
Ginger Rogers,
Kitty Foyle

Best Actor:
James Stewart,
The Philadelphia Story

Best Supporting Actress:
Jane Darwell,
The Grapes of Wrath

Best Supporting Actor:
Walter Brennan,
The Westerner

©A.M.P.A.S.®

DANCER IN THE DARK

Best Actress-winner **Ginger Rogers** left modesty in the closet when she chose this gown, which was rather risqué for the time. The lacy lingerie-style top of the dress drew attention to the dancer's bust and only competed for looks with the avalanche of diamonds dripping down her neck.

NOT YOUR BASIC BLACK

The legendary **Bette Davis's** credo was, "I dress for myself," but surely plenty of admirers were pleased by this simple yet elegant black dress. The cleavage-baring top is held up by three spaghetti straps on each shoulder, marrying design to practicality.

1942 AUSTERITY REIGNS

14TH
ACADEMY AWARDS

February 26, 1942
Biltmore Bowl
Biltmore Hotel
Los Angeles

HOST: BOB HOPE

Somber times had befallen Hollywood's most self-indulgent evening. With World War II well under way, most of the nation was dressing to reflect the grim atmosphere of the times. Out of respect for the mood of the country, the Academy issued an official request that the stars make an effort to dress more conservatively than they otherwise would on their big night. Many actresses heeded the Academy's mandate and moderated their styles to reflect the solemnity of that year.

AND THE OSCAR® GOES TO...

Best Picture:
How Green Was My Valley

Best Director:
John Ford,
How Green Was My Valley

Best Actress:
Joan Fontaine,
Suspicion

Best Actor:
Gary Cooper,
Sergeant York

Best Supporting Actress:
Mary Astor,
The Great Lie

Best Supporting Actor:
Donald Crisp,
How Green Was My Valley

©A.M.P.A.S.®

BLACK WIDOW
Best Actress-winner **Joan Fontaine** may have taken the Academy's request too far: in her black mantilla and demure jacket-like top, she looks ready to attend a funeral. The long, fitted sleeves and modestly poufed skirt are in keeping with the style of the day, but not well suited for an Academy Award-winning actress on the most glamorous night of her life.

BRIGHT SPOT
Ginger Rogers dresses up a plain, dark suit with a splash of color at her neckline. The bundle of faux flowers brightened up an otherwise subdued award show.

A HUSHED AFFAIR 1943

Patriotic fervor took hold of many of the attendees at this year's ceremony, and several speeches were made in honor of the servicemen overseas. Fittingly, the styles remained subdued, as none of the stars wanted to be viewed as preoccupied with frivolous fashions while the nation was mired in war.

15TH
ACADEMY AWARDS
March 4, 1943
The Cocoanut Grove
Ambassador Hotel
Los Angeles
HOST: BOB HOPE

AND THE OSCAR® GOES TO...

Best Picture:
Mrs. Miniver

Best Director:
William Wyler,
Mrs. Miniver

Best Actress:
Greer Garson,
Mrs. Miniver

Best Actor:
James Cagney,
Yankee Doodle Dandy

Best Supporting Actress:
Teresa Wright,
Mrs. Miniver

Best Supporting Actor:
Van Heflin,
Johnny Eager

TRIPLE PLAY

Walter Pidgeon, Greer Garson and **Ronald Colman** form a fashionable trio. Lace details and a low-cut neckline add a dash of glamour to Garson's low-key ensemble.

1944

HERE'S LOOKING AT THEM

16TH
ACADEMY AWARDS
March 2, 1944
Grauman's Chinese Theatre
Hollywood
HOST: JACK BENNY

War was still raging, so Hollywood once again went low profile as far as fashion was concerned. Men and women alike dressed down—way down. Nonetheless, there were still plenty of pretty faces to look at in the crowd at Grauman's Chinese Theatre, even if their owners were a relatively unembellished lot.

AND THE OSCAR® GOES TO...

Best Picture:
Casablanca

Best Director:
Michael Curtiz,
Casablanca

Best Actress:
Jennifer Jones,
Song of Bernadette

Best Actor:
Paul Lukas,
Watch on the Rhine

Best Supporting Actress:
Katina Paxinou,
For Whom the Bell Tolls

Best Supporting Actor:
Charles Coburn,
The More the Merrier

©A.M.P.A.S.®

VICTORY IN WARTIME

Best Actress **Jennifer Jones** and Best Supporting Actress **Katina Paxinou** beam as they clutch their Oscars. Heeding the Academy's call to observe understatement in their attire, both are dressed in tastefully modest gowns. Jones (left) wears a slim-fitting two-piece suit in the manner of 1940s daytime dressing, but makes it evening-worthy by adding a filmy, balloon-sleeved blouse underneath her suit jacket. Paxinou takes understatement to the extreme: she is quite literally draped in a jersey gown, revealing nary an inch of her skin or figure.

INGRID'S WAY 1945

With fashion still flying under the radar at the awards ceremony, all eyes were on Ingrid Bergman, the actress whose star-making turn in *Casablanca* had been snubbed the year before. Whether out of deference to the war or as part of a pointed statement to the Academy, Ingrid Bergman wore the same simple black dress to the ceremony that she had worn the year before—shocking!

17TH
ACADEMY AWARDS
March 15, 1945
Grauman's Chinese Theatre
Hollywood
HOSTS:
JOHN CROMWELL,
BOB HOPE

FRIENDLY RIVALRY

Ingrid Bergman and pal **Jennifer Jones** stand outside Grauman's Chinese Theatre on Oscar night. As was the custom in the 40s, Jones sports an elaborately detailed hat to add some pizzazz to her more subdued two-piece suit. Both wear open-toed sandals, considered very fashionable for the evening and a departure from the more popular closed-toe styles of the 30s.

©A.M.P.A.S.®

INDOOR DRESSING

An indoor shot of the two stars. Jones kept her hat on, even after removing her coat. Her suit jacket is designed in the Edwardian style. Bergman's dress (which she had worn to the previous year's ceremony) features star-like embroidery that enlivens an otherwise plain outfit.

AND THE OSCAR® GOES TO...

Best Picture:
Going My Way

Best Director:
Leo McCarey,
Going My Way

Best Actress:
Ingrid Bergman,
Gaslight

Best Actor:
Bing Crosby,
Going My Way

Best Supporting Actress:
Ethel Barrymore,
None But the Lonely Heart

Best Supporting Actor:
Barry Fitzgerald,
Going My Way

SPOTLIGHT
on Gowns: 1945

Both women wear their hair *short and curled*, in keeping with the fashion of the time.

DRAPES AND GLITTER Jane Wyman and Loretta Young are a study in contrasts. Wyman's dress is quiet and unassuming, while Young's cries out for recognition. But both of these gowns are quite modern looking, and feature design elements that are still used today.

Wyman wears a traditional two-strand *choker of pearls* over the neck of the gown.

Young's pearl choker is gathered at the throat with a hard-to-miss *decorative clasp*.

The *high collar, long sleeves and draped fit* of Wyman's gown reflect 40s ideals of modesty.

A *low neckline and cap sleeves* show off Young's necklace (and show some skin).

The monochromatic fabric of Wyman's gown places an *emphasis on cut*.

Lace trim and scattered paillettes make the gown stand out in a crowd.

A lacy V at the hips and a tulle *train* draw attention to Young's curves.

Draped material at the hips *elegantly displays* Wyman's figure.

PEACE MAKES A COMEBACK 1946

Hollywood heaved a collective sigh of relief at the end of war, and fashion at the Academy Awards bounced back in high style. The stars sparkled once again, and arrived ready to put on the type of show Hollywood is known for.

18TH
ACADEMY AWARDS
March 7, 1946
Grauman's Chinese Theatre
Hollywood

HOSTS:
JAMES STEWART,
BOB HOPE

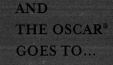

AND THE OSCAR® GOES TO...

Best Picture:
The Lost Weekend

Best Director:
Billy Wilder,
The Lost Weekend

Best Actress:
Joan Crawford,
Mildred Pierce

Best Actor:
Ray Milland,
The Lost Weekend

Best Supporting Actress:
Anne Revere, *National Velvet*

Best Supporting Actor:
James Dunn,
A Tree Grows in Brooklyn

HIS WAY

Nancy Sinatra is radiant in a full, sweeping skirt that reaches the floor, and she keeps warm with a fur coat and muff. Her husband, Frank, is wearing the male version of a glamorous1940s look, but their harmony was short-lived; the pair separated later that year.

1947 THE NEW LOOK

19TH
ACADEMY AWARDS
March 13, 1947
Shrine Auditorium
Los Angeles

HOST: JACK BENNY

After years of austerity, fashion was finally on an upswing. This was the year that Christian Dior caused a sensation in Paris by introducing his "new look": wide, generous skirts, nipped-in waists and narrow shoulders. The lavish silhouette and abundance of material necessary to create it were in extravagant contrast to the styles of the war years, and, despite some protestations about the excessive use of material, the look quickly became the new shape in fashion for the glamour set. Hollywood, of course, with its affinity for excess of all kinds, immediately embraced the look, and several stars trotted it out at that year's ceremony.

AND THE OSCAR® GOES TO...

Best Picture:
The Best Years of Our Lives

Best Director:
William Wyler,
The Best Years of Our Lives

Best Actress:
Olivia de Havilland,
To Each His Own

Best Actor:
Fredric March,
The Best Years of Our Lives

Best Supporting Actress:
Anne Baxter,
The Razor's Edge

Best Supporting Actor:
Harold Russell,
The Best Years of Our Lives

©A.M.P.A.S.®

BLUE BELLE
Best Actress-winner **Olivia de Havilland** was a sensation in a pale-blue organza gown with a meandering vine of vibrant, hand-painted flowers scattered across the skirt. The playful ruffle at the top of the bodice, colorful print and bountiful skirt seemed to say that the war was over indeed. She wisely offset the busyness of the gown with a simple choker of pearls, stud earrings and prettily coifed hair.

NO RAGGEDY ANNE
Anne Baxter receives her Best Supporting Actress Oscar in a prime example of 1940s styling. The patterned overlay of her dress dolls up a slim-fitting bodice. Her choker necklace and upswept hair are also typical of the era.
©A.M.P.A.S.®

JACKET GIRLS
Perhaps not quite ready to let go of the buttoned-down austerity of the previous years, both **Cathy O'Donnell** (who accepted the Best Actor award for Fredric March) and **Joan Fontaine** are wearing short jackets with their Oscar outfits. Fontaine's jacket, with its glittering beadwork and mandarin collar, is unusual for the era, and foreshadows a look that is to become more common in the 1960s.
©A.M.P.A.S.®

COSTUMER'S COMEUPPANCE *1948*

While many of Hollywood's stars were taking advantage of the opportunity that the end of war gave them to grab the limelight and show off their most glamorous looks, there were plenty of behind-the-scenes tastemakers still toiling in obscurity. To remedy the problem, this was the year that Hollywood added a new category to its roster of awards, that of Best Costume Design. It seemed appropriate that an industry that relied so much on appearances should finally give credit to the very people who helped make movies the magical spectacles they were. As if in support of the debuting award, and with the new, flashier look of fashion still emerging, the stars arrived in high style.

20TH
ACADEMY AWARDS
March 20, 1948
Shrine Auditorium
Los Angeles
HOSTS:
AGNES MOOREHEAD
DICK POWELL

©A.M.P.A.S.®

GREEN FLASH
Surprise Best Actress-winner **Loretta Young** swept into the awards ceremony swathed in tufts of emerald-green silk taffeta. The yards of material needed to craft the ruffles, folds and other embellishments represent the very embodiment of fashion's new look of plenty. Not one known for her sartorial subtlety, Young topped off the dress with an equally opulent diamond necklace. .

STATUESQUE BEAUTY
In the antithesis of Young's outfit, presenter **Ingrid Bergman** wore a gown draped in the manner of classic Grecian sculptures. The generous folds and fluttering sleeves add to the charm of the look, as does her boyish, non-"done" hairstyle. Bergman, with her natural beauty and dignified look, is probably one of the few actresses who could have pulled off this enchanting look.

©A.M.P.A.S.®

**AND
THE OSCAR®
GOES TO...**

**Best Picture/
Best Director:**
Elia Kazan,
Gentleman's Agreement

Best Actress:
Loretta Young,
The Farmer's Daughter

Best Actor:
Ronald Colman,
A Double Life

Best Supporting Actress:
Celeste Holm,
Gentleman's Agreement

Best Supporting Actor:
Edmund Gwenn,
Miracle on 34th Street

39

1949

GOODBYE TO ALL THAT

21ST
ACADEMY AWARDS
March 24, 1949
The Academy Theatre
Hollywood

HOST:
GEORGE
MONTGOMERY

Fashion continued to evolve as the decade came to a close. The 1949 ceremony represented a mishmash of styles, with stars looking forward and back. Some came dressed in the slim-fitting sheaths of the 40s, while others wore fuller gowns that foreshadowed the more glamorous styles of the 50s that were soon to come.

AND THE OSCAR® GOES TO...

Best Picture:
Hamlet

Best Director:
John Huston,
The Treasure of the Sierra Madre

Best Actress:
Jane Wyman,
Johnny Belinda

Best Actor:
Laurence Olivier,
Hamlet

Best Supporting Actress:
Claire Trevor,
Key Largo

Best Supporting Actor:
Walter Huston,
The Treasure of the Sierra Madre

STOLEN GLANCES
Swathed in a fur stole over a fitted gown, **Jane Russell's** glamorous look is a harbinger of styles to come.

©A.M.P.A.S.®

LACED IN
Presenter **Jeanne Crain's** strapless gown hints at the look of the coming decade: the fitted bodice and flared skirt would become one of the most popular silhouettes of the 1950s, as Dior's "new look" dominated the fashion scene in Hollywood. The matching lace bolero she wears on her shoulders would become a popular feature of wedding gowns in the coming decade.

GAL PALS
Loretta Young (right) congratulates Best Actress-winner **Jane Wyman** on her Oscar. Wyman, who had recently divorced from future-president Ronald Reagan, is wrapped in a slim sheath, echoing the slim, fitted look that was popular in the 40s. The classic gown recalls the subtle drape of the gown Ingrid Bergman wore the year before, while its low waist is reminiscent of the flapper dresses of the 20s. Young's frillier gown, adorned with lace and spangles, is an example of the fun women were having in dressing more extravagantly after the hard times of the war years had passed.

©A.M.P.A.S.®

AND OSCAR MAKES THREE

Sometimes, even if an actress arrives at the Oscars with her significant other, he and she aren't the only ones waltzing down the red carpet — a few women have attended the Oscars with babies in utero. With their due dates looming, these women made the most of their curvaceous figures on their, ahem, "big" nights.

2003
AND ALL THAT JAZZ

Catherine Zeta-Jones, nominated for Best Supporting Actress in *Chicago*, was eight and one-half months pregnant when she went onstage to collect her Oscar. She even performed a duet from the film with Queen Latifah. But for the rest of the night she sat in an aisle seat; hubby Michael Douglas had made sure an ambulance was parked outside the Kodak Theatre, just in case the big moment arrived during the ceremony.

1955
BREAKING THE WATERFRONT

Eva Marie Saint made it to the Oscars despite being more than eight months pregnant. After winning an Oscar for her performance in *On the Waterfront*, she told the audience, "I'm so excited I might even have my baby right here!" Actually, she had the baby the next day.

2000
AMERICAN BEAUTY

Annette Bening attended the Oscars on the very day her baby was due. She sat with husband Warren Beatty in the second row while host Billy Crystal looked at them and quipped, "Something they produced together may be released tonight."

1991
IN FULL BLOOM

Denzel Washington's wife, Pauletta, was blooming like a buttercup in this pretty yellow gown with glittering bodice. The off-the-shoulder neckline was so flattering it might have momentarily distracted fans from her bulging belly.

THE *1950s*

FAR FROM HEAVEN

With the austere war years far behind, the nation was enjoying a new era of affluence, and no one was better equipped to show off the extravagant new look of luxury than the stars of Hollywood. The economy was thriving and luxury goods flooded the market, heralding a national obsession with "the good life." Women across the country aspired to a life in which they could be pampered, or at least dress to show the world that they were well taken care of by their husbands. Those who could afford it dressed in coveted luxury materials like silks, satins and furs. Innovations in fabric technology allowed garments to be dyed in vivid new shades, giving clothes a rich look that echoed the nation's prosperity. Celebrities lived the life that women everywhere dreamed of, and Oscar night was the time to prove it. Style icons like Audrey Hepburn and Grace Kelly represented one ideal, that of prim perfection, with their trim figures and proper manners. But the voluptuous, hourglass figures of actresses like Marilyn Monroe and Elizabeth Taylor most embodied the look of plenty that had the nation entranced. These bountiful stars were embraced by a public hungry for abundance in all its forms.

FASHION ON FILM

All About Eve (1950)

All About Eve showed moviegoers the glamorous side of life in the 1950s—and who better to represent the era than Bette Davis and Marilyn Monroe? Monroe's gown is a confectionary treat, with its gathered bodice and gauzy skirt festooned with a silk flower, while Davis gives off an air of stately elegance in her bold, off-the-shoulder cocktail dress.

Sabrina (1954)

It's hard to say what was more popular in this film: the rising star Audrey Hepburn, or the clothes she wore. Her collaboration with French designer Hubert de Givenchy resulted in one of the most influential film wardrobes of all time. Several of today's fashion mainstays were first spotted in this film, including the classic Sabrina dress and what are now called Sabrina heels.

DESIGNERS TO THE STARS: 1950s

LOUIS FÉRAUD (1920-1999)

Le Vie en Rose

Because Louis Féraud opened his boutique in Cannes, not Paris, he was considered something of a fashion outsider. But when Hollywood stars began arriving en masse in Cannes for the film festival, this little-known designer became a star in his own right. Féraud created vibrant, frilly, fun dresses and gowns, and was a favorite of sex-kitten Brigitte Bardot, as well as Ingrid Bergman, Elizabeth Taylor, Grace Kelly and Kim Novak. He was so popular with actresses, in fact, that he ended up designing costumes for over 20 films, including the French film *En Cas de Malheur*, which starred Bardot.

CHRISTIAN DIOR (1905-1957)

The Godfather

Christian Dior was one of the most influential designers of all time. He caused a sensation when he launched his 1947 collection in Paris, immediately dubbed the "new look" by fashion insiders. He went to great lengths (literally) to revive "French luxury," designing voluminous gowns that emphasized slender waists and full busts. Narrow shoulders, nipped-in waists and full, broad skirts were all Dior hallmarks imitated far and wide. His designs were favored by leading Hollywood stars, including Grace Kelly, Greta Garbo and Marlene Dietrich. Tragically, he died a mere decade after transforming fashion forever, but his legacy lives on to this day.

OLEG CASSINI (1913–)

Designer and Lover

Born in Paris to Russian parents, Oleg Cassini began his career as an assistant wardrobe designer in Hollywood before striking out on his own. He dressed actress Gene Tierney, and the two later married. When that marriage ended, he met and fell in love with Grace Kelly, for whom he also designed and to whom he was briefly engaged. Later, Cassini would come to be known as the private couturier to First Lady Jacqueline Kennedy. Once the First Lady became his muse and model, his designs were admired and copied by an entire nation of women.

1950 NEW AWAKENINGS

Full, floor-length skirts, belted waists, splashes of color and vibrant accents like flowers suffused the air with the sense that fashion was waking up from a long slumber. Hollywood's A list turned out in charming ensembles that eschewed the meager rationing of the previous decade and finally allowed the stars to have some fun.

22ND
ACADEMY AWARDS
March 23, 1950
Pantages Theater
Hollywood
HOST:
PAUL DOUGLAS

AND THE OSCAR® GOES TO...

Best Picture:
All the King's Men

Best Director:
Joseph L. Mankiewicz,
A Letter to Three Wives

Best Actress:
Olivia de Havilland,
The Heiress

Best Actor:
Broderick Crawford,
All the King's Men

Best Supporting Actress:
Mercedes McCambridge,
All the King's Men

Best Supporting Actor:
Dean Jagger,
Twelve O'Clock High

©A.M.P.A.S.®

BLOOMING BEAUTY

Though she won the Oscar for playing a frumpy heiress, **Olivia de Havilland** looked anything but dowdy in this belted evening dress festooned with flowers. The last time she won the Oscar, in 1947, she also wore a floral-themed dress, but the flowers then were painted on; this time, they look as if they're ready to be plucked, representing the new exuberance of fashion—and the nation.

LUCKY STRIKE

Best Supporting Actress **Mercedes McCambridge** is said to have worn her dress, which was thirteen years old, for luck. Apparently the strapless, full-length gown with matching handless gloves worked like a charm. With her is Best Supporting Actor-winner **Dean Jagger**.

©A.M.P.A.S.®

AMERICA'S SWEETHEART

June Allyson is pretty as a picture as she presents the Oscar for Best Cinematography. Her gown features spaghetti straps holding up a heart-shaped neckline, a gathered bust, and a full, flared skirt, in keeping with the silhouette of the time. At her waist, a corsage of fabricated flowers makes the look more playful.

©A.M.P.A.S.®

BOX-OFFICE BLOWOUT 1951

1950 was the worst year in the history of Hollywood as box-office receipts fell to an all-time low. The meager turnout at theaters was mostly attributed to the advent of television and the new popular pastime of staying home to watch it. Undeterred, the stars still dressed as if they were on top of the world, and sure enough, Hollywood's box-office woes soon passed.

23RD
ACADEMY AWARDS
March 29, 1951
Pantages Theater
Hollywood
HOST: FRED ASTAIRE

©A.M.P.A.S.®

NATURAL GLOW

Jane Greer dazzles in this gown embellished with sequins. The sparkling trail seems to wrap around the actress's curves like clinging vines. The slinky look of this gown is more in keeping with 1940s styles than the over-the-top glamour that was soon to dominate 50s dressing. With her is presenter **George Pol**.

AND THE OSCAR® GOES TO...

Best Picture:
All About Eve

Best Director:
Joseph L. Mankiewicz,
All About Eve

Best Actress:
Judy Holliday,
Born Yesterday

Best Actor:
José Ferrer,
Cyrano de Bergerac

Best Supporting Actress:
Josephine Hull, *Harvey*

Best Supporting Actor:
George Sanders,
All About Eve

1952
ALL QUIET ON THE OSCAR FRONT

Fashion continued to find itself at the Academy Awards in 1952. Perhaps because they weren't making a huge splash at the theaters, the ensembles the stars wore to the ceremony were a relatively tame lot. All that would change in the next year, when the Oscars were broadcast on television for the first time.

24TH
ACADEMY AWARDS
March 20, 1952
Pantages Theater
Hollywood
HOST: DANNY KAYE

AND THE OSCAR® GOES TO...

Best Picture:
An American in Paris

Best Director:
George Stevens,
A Place in the Sun

Best Actress:
Vivien Leigh,
A Streetcar Named Desire

Best Actor:
Humphrey Bogart,
The African Queen

Best Supporting Actress:
Kim Hunter,
A Streetcar Named Desire

Best Supporting Actor:
Karl Malden,
A Streetcar Named Desire

©A.M.P.A.S.®

A STAND-UP GAL

In a departure from the usual style of dressing, **Claire Trevor** wears an unusual evening gown printed with a natural motif of vines and leaves. A flourish of fabric, not unlike flora of some sort itself, adorns her left shoulder strap, but her elbow-length evening gloves and strands of pearls ground the gown in the traditional style of 1950s attire. **Karl Malden** is with her.

©A.M.P.A.S.®

A PARISIAN IN HOLLYWOOD

Leslie Caron (French star of *An American in Paris*) poses with the Oscar for Best Foreign Language Production awarded to Ken Yoshida. Caron's gown is quite risqué—the bodice appears to fall down of its own accord to reveal a lacy piece of lingerie underneath. In reality the gown was constructed to look this way. The strapless bodice and lavish skirt of the gown are clearly influenced by fellow Parisian Christian Dior's "new look."

LIVE, FROM LOS ANGELES!

1953

In an effort to revive popular interest in film and bring audiences back to the movie theaters, in 1953, the Academy Awards were broadcast on television for the first time. This was the year the general public would finally get the chance to participate in the Oscar ceremonies and live the Hollywood dream, albeit vicariously. Not surprisingly, the stars dressed to the hilt, in opulent outfits that would show the television audience just what Hollywood was all about. Edith Head, a longtime costume designer at Paramount, was even appointed official fashion consultant to prevent Hollywood's elite from making any sartorial missteps. She was also responsible for keeping the stars decent: she covered up cleavage and dimmed down diamonds. Nonetheless, the stars still dazzled, and the event was the most watched television program of all time.

25TH
ACADEMY AWARDS
March 19, 1953
Pantages Theater
Hollywood
HOST: BOB HOPE

AND THE OSCAR® GOES TO...

Best Picture:
The Greatest Show on Earth

Best Director:
John Ford,
The Quiet Man

Best Actress:
Shirley Booth,
Come Back, Little Sheba

Best Actor:
Gary Cooper, *High Noon*

Best Supporting Actress:
Gloria Grahame,
The Bad and the Beautiful

Best Supporting Actor:
Anthony Quinn,
Viva Zapata!

©A.M.P.A.S.®

NOT SHORT ON STYLE

Jane Wyman steals the spotlight as she co-presents the Academy Award for Short Subjects. Her full-skirted gown with apron overlay is an enthralling example of lavish 1950s styling. (Some gowns from this era had hems with circumferences of up to 12 feet.) The fitted bodice, tulle shawl and pearl choker intensify the glam factor of this terrific ensemble. With her is **Ray Milland**.

PAYING THE PIPER

Piper Laurie accepts the Oscar on behalf of **T.E.B. Clarke**, who wrote *The Lavender Hill Mob*. Laurie is the epitome of 1950s glamour in a satin gown with full skirt and pearl-encrusted bodice with low neckline.

ALL LACED UP

Joan Fontaine's two-toned dress, with its wide, bell-shaped skirt, cinched and belted waist, and softly sloping shoulders, was, like other dresses under the influence of Dior's "new look," reminiscent of the belle époque. Befitting the needs of an actress, the lacy capelet adds drama and flair to the popular style.

1954 FULL SPEED AHEAD

Fashion gained a foothold at the Oscars this year as actresses began arriving in some of the decade's most interesting creations yet. Full skirts and lavish styling reflected the prosperity the nation was feeling.

26TH
ACADEMY AWARDS
March 25, 1954
Pantages Theater
Hollywood
HOST: BOB HOPE

AND THE OSCAR® GOES TO...

Best Picture:
From Here to Eternity

Best Director:
Fred Zinnemann,
From Here to Eternity

Best Actress:
Audrey Hepburn,
Roman Holiday

Best Actor:
William Holden,
Stalag 17

Best Supporting Actress:
Donna Reed,
From Here to Eternity

Best Supporting Actor:
Frank Sinatra,
From Here to Eternity

©A.M.P.A.S.®

CLASSIC BEAUTY

Best Actress-winner **Audrey Hepburn** exemplifies the look of 1950s chic in this belted floral dress by her close friend, the designer Hubert de Givenchy. The bateau neckline was an unusual choice for an Oscar dress, but it suits the gamine Ms. Hepburn perfectly. For jewelry, the star wore only small teardrop earrings.

©A.M.P.A.S.®

GLAMOUR GIRLS

Best Supporting Actress **Donna Reed** and presenter **Mercedes McCambridge** show off the look of 1950s glamour. The fitted bodices with built-in boning for support, lavishly full skirts and ethereal fabrics are wonderful examples of 1950s styling. Don't be fooled by the light and frothy look of the gowns—before the invention of lighter, synthetic fabrics, several yards of heavy material were often used to create the luxuriant look of gowns such as these, and stiff petticoats were often worn underneath the bouffant skirts to give them their weightless look. Note the lace cummerbund at the waist of McCambridge's gown—yet another way to show off a trim figure. **Frank Sinatra** is between them.

SCENE STEALERS 1955

The spotlight shone on some of the most glamorous gowns in the world at 1955's Oscars. Actresses took full advantage of the ultra-feminine looks of the 1950s and paraded at this year's Oscars in some of the finest clothing yet seen.

27TH
ACADEMY AWARDS
March 30, 1955
Pantages Theater
Hollywood
HOST: BOB HOPE

PLAYING AGAINST TYPE

Donna Reed breaks out of her role as the ideal 1950s housewife and gets glammed-up in this strapless gown featuring a heavily boned and shirred bodice and a gathered and flounced skirt. A matching scarf hangs seductively from her neck, partially obscuring an elaborate diamond necklace. With her is Best Supporting Actor **Edmond O'Brien**.

AND THE OSCAR® GOES TO...

Best Picture:
On the Waterfront

Best Director:
Elia Kazan,
On the Waterfront

Best Actress:
Grace Kelly, *The Country Girl*

Best Actor:
Marlon Brando,
On the Waterfront

Best Supporting Actress:
Eva Marie Saint,
On the Waterfront

Best Supporting Actor:
Edmond O'Brien,
The Barefoot Contessa

INTRODUCING DOROTHY DANDRIDGE

A stunning **Dorothy Dandridge** sweeps into the Oscars in a hip-skimming sheath with long, fitted sleeves and a deep V-neck. A fur stole adds just the right touch of sophistication. Though Dandridge never won an Oscar, she helped pave the way for other African American actresses, such as Halle Berry, who the Best Actress Oscar in 2002. Berry also won a Golden Globe for playing Dandridge in the 1999 TV film, *Introducing Dorothy Dandridge*.

©A.M.P.A.S.®

FIT FOR A PRINCESS

This blue-champagne silk gown with spaghetti straps and a subtly draped waist is one of the most beautiful Oscar gowns of all time. Designer Edith Head claimed the fabric was specially woven in Paris and that it alone cost $4,000. The gown was undoubtedly rendered even more breathtaking because it was worn by that year's Best Actress-winner, **Grace Kelly**.

SPOTLIGHT
on Gowns: EARLY 1950s

PIPER LAURIE BOLD LUXURY

Piper Laurie embodies the luxurious, decorous look of the 1950s. Her ensemble was carefully orchestrated with all the trimmings of the 1950s look, almost as if she were donning a uniform. The outfit combined all the elements of the look of luxury that prompted oohs and aahs from women across the country on Oscar night.

A three-strand *pearl choker*—pearls aren't as flashy as diamonds, but they have enough luster to show the world that the wearer appreciates understated good taste, and has the money to say so.

Nothing spelled luxury more than a *fur stole*. This one looks exceptionally soft and as pure as the driven snow— just like the wearer, no doubt! (Or at least she would have us think …)

A *pearl-encrusted bodice* and *tasteful décolletage*. These days, only a young bride would wear a gown like this, but back in the 50s, opulence ruled the night.

Long, white *evening gloves*. The easiest shortcut to elegance.

A *full, round skirt*, preferably in a shimmering fabric like silk or satin. Yards and yards of fabric were the epitome of style — or at least that's what high fashion led the world to believe during the decade.

AUDREY HEPBURN
TASTEFUL ELEGANCE

Audrey Hepburn was fashion forward enough to forego the obvious trappings of evening wear and forged a look that was uniquely her own. With the help of designer Hubert de Givenchy, she consistently donned some of the chicest outfits in all of Hollywood. This ensemble is just one example of her impeccable taste.

A *pixie haircut* with chunky, short bangs framed her delicate face and showed off her huge doe eyes.

A *bateau neckline* shows off Hepburn's clavicles and long, graceful neck. Unlike the more common low-cut necklines, this one projects innocence.

Hepburn's tiny midsection is accentuated by a *cinched-in waist*. The belt is made of the same fabric as the gown.

The *full skirt* of this dress flows away from the tiny waist like an inverted funnel. The full-skirted effect is pretty and girlish, and extremely flattering. The hem lands at about mid-calf, well above floor-length, so as not to trip up girls on the go.

1956

THE CLOTHES ARE THE THING

As the Oscars' ceremonies became more popular to viewers at home, the awards show subtly transformed itself into a spectacle that was as much about fashion as it was about winners and losers. The attendees kept up appearances by continuing to don ever-changing and increasingly daring outfits.

28TH
ACADEMY AWARDS
March 21, 1956
Pantages Theater
Hollywood
HOST: JERRY LEWIS

AND THE OSCAR® GOES TO...

Best Picture:
Marty

Best Director:
Delbert Mann, *Marty*

Best Actress:
Anna Magnani,
The Rose Tattoo

Best Actor:
Ernest Borgnine, *Marty*

Best Supporting Actress:
Jo Van Fleet, *East of Eden*

Best Supporting Actor:
Jack Lemmon,
Mister Roberts

©A.M.P.A.S.®

AT THE FOREFRONT

A year after giving birth, presenter **Eva Marie Saint** easily fits into a satin gown with flowing skirt. The peplumed bodice adorned with delicate buttons lend this gown a unique look not seen on other stars. Alongside her is **Jack Lemmon**, who took home the award for Best Supporting Actor.

©A.M.P.A.S.®

ALL WRAPPED UP

Resplendent in a gown designed by MGM Studio's Helen Rose, presenter **Grace Kelly** gets wrapped in light-as-air organdy scattered with flowers. The future princess wears short gloves with scalloped edges to complement this enchanting look.

FLEET-FOOTED

Best Supporting Actress-winner **Jo Van Fleet** celebrates her victory in a pleated tulle gown with scoop-neck bodice, a simple pearl necklace, and elbow-length white gloves. **Audrey Hepburn** is charming in her demure polka-dotted dress with wide shoulder straps. Her simple elegance calls only for large pearl earrings and evening gloves that reach far beyond her elbows. Best Actor-winner **Ernest Borgnine** stands between the two beauties.

©A.M.P.A.S.®

STAR POWER 1957

As the decade rolled to a close, fashions were getting so sexy and the stars were wearing them so well that the show's producers started receiving complaints about the amount of cleavage being shown on live television. The next year, a memo was even sent out asking the show's wardrobe managers to keep the stars' necklines at a more appropriate level.

29TH
ACADEMY AWARDS
March 27, 1957
Pantages Theater, Hollywood;
NBC Century Theater,
New York
HOSTS: JERRY LEWIS AND
CELESTE HOLM

©A.M.P.A.S.®

SUPPORTING A BIG GRIN

Best Supporting Actress-winner **Dorothy Malone** clutches her Oscar in gloved hands. She chose a gown with a deep, off-the-shoulder collar, balloon sleeves and tiny buttons on the torso, all the better to frame her face. With her is Best Supporting Actor-winner **Anthony Quinn**.

AND THE OSCAR® GOES TO...

Best Picture:
Around the World in 80 Days

Best Director:
George Stevens,
Giant

Best Actress:
Ingrid Bergman,
Anastasia

Best Actor:
Yul Brynner,
The King and I

Best Supporting Actress:
Dorothy Malone,
Written on the Wind

Best Supporting Actor:
Anthony Quinn,
Lust for Life

QUEEN FOR A NIGHT

©A.M.P.A.S.®

A regal **Elizabeth Taylor**, tiara and all, holds court with husband **Mike Todd**, who had just won the Best Picture Oscar for his film *Around the World in Eighty Days*. Taylor's shirred chiffon gown features a spaghetti-strap on the left shoulder and a twist of fabric secured with a brooch on the right. In addition to the diamond tiara, her ears are hung with huge diamond earrings. They were given to her by her husband, who would die almost a year later in a plane crash. Presenter **Janet Gaynor** looks on.

WHITE SHOULDERS

A captivating **Natalie Wood** arrives at the Oscars wearing an off-the-shoulder satin gown exposing her creamy neck, which she leaves unadorned. A fur stole trimmed with feathers and evening gloves are all the embellishments she needs.

1958

GLAMOUR AMID GRIEF

Three major Hollywood players all died in the week before this year's awards show, including Elizabeth Taylor's husband, producer Mike Todd. But the ceremony itself went off without a hitch, and was one of the most glamorous and star-studded events yet.

30TH
ACADEMY AWARDS
March 26, 1958
Pantages Theater
Hollywood
HOSTS: VARIOUS

AND THE OSCAR® GOES TO...

Best Picture:
The Bridge on the River Kwai

Best Director:
David Lean,
The Bridge on the River Kwai

Best Actress:
Joanne Woodward,
The Three Faces of Eve

Best Actor:
Alec Guinness,
The Bridge on the River Kwai

Best Supporting Actress:
Miyoshi Umeki, *Sayonara*

Best Supporting Actor:
Red Buttons, *Sayonara*

©A.M.P.A.S.®

GARDEN PARTY

Jean Simmons (shown with **Cary Grant** holding the Oscar awarded to Alec Guinness for his performance in *The Bridge on the River Kwai*) chose a delightful strapless gown in satin with strips of fabric running across like latticework in a garden. The cluster of fabricated flowers at thigh level adds a touch of romance to this fanciful gown. Note the bunch of simple bangles on her left wrist, an unusual choice in Oscar-night jewelry.

©A.M.P.A.S.®

WOODWARD'S OWN

Recently wed to the handsome Paul Newman, **Joanne Woodward** caused a stir by designing her own dress, and with fabric she bought for just $100. Slightly ill-fitting around the bodice, the homemade gown prompted Joan Crawford to comment, "Joanne Woodward is setting the cause of glamour back by twenty years."

54

OUT WITH A BANG 1959

The final year of the decade was a veritable pageant of styles from the 50s, with stars still representing an innocence that would disappear in the decade to come. Of course, no one yet had any idea of what was in store for them with the advent of the swinging 60s, and many of the pearl-wearing, gloved ladies at the Oscars would surely be in a for a shock.

31ST
ACADEMY AWARDS
April 6, 1959
Pantages Theater
Hollywood
HOSTS: VARIOUS

©A.M.P.A.S.®

AND THE OSCAR® GOES TO...

Best Picture/Director:
Vincente Minnelli, *Gigi*

Best Actress:
Susan Hayward,
I Want to Live!

Best Actor:
David Niven,
Separate Tables

Best Supporting Actress:
Wendy Hiller,
Separate Tables

Best Supporting Actor:
Burl Ives, *The Big Country*

ALL BUTTONED UP

Compared to most of the stars at that night's ceremony, **Millie Perkins** looks exceedingly modest in her suit-like gown with proper buttons down the front and a wide boat neck. Even her jewelry is barely detectable—she wears nothing but small pearls in her ears. With her is Best Director **Vincent Minnelli**.

©A.M.P.A.S.®

TIP OF THE HAT

Presenter **Ingrid Bergman** gets a tip of the cap from actor **Maurice Chevalier**, decked out in a morning suit complete with top hat. Bergman wears the type of dress that personified the 50s, with its brocade, boat-neck bodice, cinched and belted waist, and full, calf-length skirt.

OSCAR ELEGANCE

Best Actress-winner **Susan Hayward** glows in this simple yet fetching gown. Note how the fabric—embroidered with a flower-like motif—looks strikingly similar to that of Joanne Woodward's gown of the previous year.

©A.M.P.A.S.®

REPEAT PERFORMANCES

I n fashion, as in life, what goes around comes around. Just take a look at these Oscar-night ensembles. They were designed by different people and worn by different stars, sometimes decades apart, but in all of them you can detect a steadfast style that has survived the passing of the years and flash-in-the-pan trends. While fads may come and go, one thing is here to stay: beautiful, flattering clothes that help make Hollywood look its best.

THE LOOK: The Floral Print
THE TIME LAPSE: 33 years

Vivien Leigh wore her floral print gown to accept her Academy Award for Best Actress in *Gone with the Wind* in 1940. Thirty-three years later, **Natalie Wood** wore a very similar dress as a 1973 presenter. Not only are the prints on the gowns similar, but the sundress-like straps and low-cut décolletage follow almost exactly the same pattern. If they took off their jewelry, both of these actresses would be ready for a picnic!

1973

©A.M.P.A.S.®

1940

THE LOOK: Shiny Tuxedos
THE TIME LAPSE: 26 years

Diana Ross wore a pop-star-worthy silver satin tuxedo with a rhinestone vest and black ascot, designed by Bob Mackie. Almost three decades later, **Angelina Jolie** donned a more refined version of the shiny menswear trend in this Dolce & Gabbana white pantsuit. She opted to leave off the vest, shirt and ascot, and went for a sexy, cleavage-baring look. This is definitely not your father's tuxedo.

1975

2001

©A.M.P.A.S.®

In a one-shouldered, one-sleeved gown that she designed herself, **Anjelica Huston's** fashion statement was undoubtedly unique as she accepted her Oscar for *Prizzi's Honor* in 1986. But 17 years later, fellow Oscar-winner **Marcia Gay Harden** "honored" the look once again in this brilliant turquoise gown with only one shoulder strap. In addition to their asymmetry and vivid, sea-worthy tones, both gowns also featured a ruched bust.

©A.M.P.A.S.®

926

1986

2003

2001

THE LOOK: Flapper Girl
THE TIME LAPSE: 75 years!

Apparently, some fashions really stand the test of time. **Juliette Binoche** mimicked the look of silent-screen star **Gloria Swanson** and other 1920s flappers by wearing multiple strands of pearls around her neck and putting marcel curls in her hair.

THE *1960s*

BACK TO THE FUTURE

If the 1950s, with their ultrafeminine, full skirts-and-pearls uniform, were all about looking backward, then the 1960s were about looking forward. The studios loosened their hold on what the stars could wear to the Oscars just as women across the country began shedding their restrictive, voluminous skirts and dresses in favor of clothing that allowed more freedom of movement: curves were straightened, and hemlines shot up. Although Hollywood was one of the last bastions of glamour to get in line with the new direction fashion was taking, even the most sophisticated of stars couldn't help but wear clothes imbued with the look of the future—even the haute couture houses were making clothes influenced by street fashion, as youth culture began to dominate the popular imagination for the first time. Freedom was, after all, one of the major themes of the 60s, and it's no surprise that fashion began to reflect this ideal. The elegant women of previous decades were suddenly seen as square and stodgy. Brigitte Bardot was said to have rebuffed the *grande dame* of women's fashion, Coco Chanel, when Chanel offered to give the young starlet lessons in elegance. Other young stars were among the first to try out new looks on the red carpet. There was revolution among the masses, and slowly but surely, Hollywood began to catch on.

Breakfast at Tiffany's (1961)

Audrey Hepburn's Holly Golightly character inspired millions to find the perfect little black dress and a few strands of pearls to go with it. Her long cigarette holder and black gloves also became symbols of the ultimate in chic looks for women.

Bonnie and Clyde (1967)

Even though she played a ruthless killer, Faye Dunaway's classic beauty onscreen made women want to look just like her character. Dunaway's gangster moll generated a huge street trend called the "Bonnie look" that spurred thousands of young women to don berets, neckerchiefs and skirts (but, thankfully, no gun).

DESIGNERS TO THE STARS: 1960s

HUBERT DE GIVENCHY (1927–)

Simply Chic

Hubert de Givenchy is perhaps best known as Audrey Hepburn's close friend and personal designer. He created Hepburn's wardrobe for the film *Breakfast at Tiffany's*, which remains one of the most influential films, stylewise, of all time. Givenchy learned at the feet of masters like Balenciaga, who taught the younger designer about craftsmanship. But Givenchy was never as somber as the great Spanish couturier; he made his mark on fashion by creating clothes that were chic, simple, sophisticated and extremely wearable in everyday life. Many of the looks he developed with Hepburn, like the big, white menswear shirt, Capris and ballet flats, remain staples in women's closets to this day.

YVES SAINT LAURENT (1936–)

Fashion Genius

Deemed by some the genius of the century, Yves Saint Laurent took over the house of Dior after the death of its namesake in 1957. Fashionistas everywhere held their breath: would the 21-year-old wunderkind ring the death knell for haute couture? The naysayers needn't have worried. Saint Laurent went on to design some of the most innovative, beautiful clothes the world had ever seen. Not only could he keep up the tradition of creating gorgeous gowns that had elevated dressmaking to the level of art, he was also a master at translating street fashion into something well-dressed women clamored to wear. He was the first designer to bring to high fashion the ethnic looks that hippies coveted, and he developed a way of designing women's pants suits that made them as sensual as the slinkiest gown. French actress Catherine Deneuve was his friend and muse.

PACO RABANNE (1934–)

Ahead of His Time

It was the era of man's first flight to the moon, and no designer was more influenced by the Space Age than Paco Rabanne. Forgoing needle and thread, he created futuristic dresses made out of alternative materials like leather patches, aluminum rivets, ostrich feathers, plastic disks linked by hooks, even chain mail. His forward-looking designs became even more popular when he created the barely-there costumes Jane Fonda wore in *Barbarella*. Suddenly, the idea of a sexy space girl became the image starlets everywhere aspired to.

*19*60 STILL PRIM AND PROPER

Ben-Hur **stole the show this year**, which is more than can be said for the fashions. In the first year of the decade, most stars were still stuck in the 1950s, arriving in the same prim attire they'd been wearing the year before.

32ND
ACADEMY AWARDS
April 4, 1960
Pantages Theater
Hollywood
HOST: BOB HOPE

AND
THE OSCAR®
GOES TO...

Best Picture:
Ben-Hur

Best Director:
William Wyler, *Ben-Hur*

Best Actress:
Simone Signoret,
Room at the Top

Best Actor:
Charlton Heston, *Ben-Hur*

Best Supporting Actress:
Shelley Winters,
The Diary of Anne Frank

Best Supporting Actor:
Hugh Griffith, *Ben-Hur*

COLD HANDS
Best Supporting Actress-winner **Shelley Winters** can be forgiven for not being fashion forward, because this gown is such a prime example of 1950s styling. Every element of the uniform is here: the pearl choker, elbow-length gloves, ruched bodice with nipped-in waist and full, generous skirt. She's even got a fur stole hidden behind her back, which should be enough to keep her warm.

KILLER OUTFIT
Not everyone was dressed in last years clothes. *Psycho* star **Janet Leigh** (with husband Tony Curtis) dazzles in this belted, fitted dress. The white gloves provide the requisite evening elegance, but the close fit and brilliant sparkle of the fabric are very modern for the time.

MAY I HAVE THIS DANCE? 1961

A year later, the stars were no closer to shedding the uniform of the past decade. Even the usually sexy Elizabeth Taylor looked dressed to attend her senior prom—and no, that's not a hickey on her neck, but a scar from her recent tracheotomy.

33RD
ACADEMY AWARDS
April 17, 1961
Santa Monica Civic Auditorium
Santa Monica
HOST: BOB HOPE

©A.M.P.A.S.®

©A.M.P.A.S.®

AND THE OSCAR® GOES TO...

Best Picture:
The Apartment

Best Director:
Billy Wilder, *The Apartment*

Best Actress:
Elizabeth Taylor, *BUtterfield 8*

Best Actor:
Burt Lancaster, *Elmer Gantry*

Best Supporting Actress:
Shirley Jones, *Elmer Gantry*

Best Supporting Actor:
Peter Ustinov, *Spartacus*

PRINCESS FOR A DAY

Dripping with baubles, Best Supporting Actress-winner **Shirley Jones** gets bussed by Hugh Griffith. Her frothy concoction of a dress personifies an era that is about to pass, that of movie stars dressing like princesses to attend the Academy Awards. Soon stars would be adopting a sleeker look that would endure to this day.

PETAL PUSHER

Despite having flown directly from a hospital in London to the ceremony, **Elizabeth Taylor** looks fresh as a rose in this demure Dior gown that keeps her famous bosom under wraps. The boat neck and bow around her waist, festooned with a giant silk flower, lend her a sweet and proper look—quite a departure from her many glamorous getups.

©A.M.P.A.S.®

SAINTLY LOOK

Eva Marie Saint holds an Oscar presented to Peter Ustinov for his Best Supporting Actor performance in *Spartacus*. Unlike the unusual gown she donned in 1955, she took no chances with this conservative strapless gown with matching evening gloves.

19*62* IN THE HEAT OF THE NIGHT

Things began to heat up this year, as stars finally started breaking out of the cookie-cutter mold of the 1950s. Ann-Margret wowed the crowd in her sexy, sleek gown, and Natalie Wood was ravishing in white satin.

34TH
ACADEMY AWARDS
April 9, 1962
Santa Monica Civic Auditorium
Santa Monica
HOST: BOB HOPE

AND THE OSCAR® GOES TO...

Best Picture:
West Side Story

Best Director:
Robert Wise and Jerome Robbins, *West Side Story*

Best Actress:
Sophia Loren, *Two Women*

Best Actor:
Maximilian Schell, *Judgment at Nuremberg*

Best Supporting Actress:
Rita Moreno, *West Side Story*

Best Supporting Actor:
George Chakiris, *West Side Story*

SPLENDOR IN SILK

Best Actress-nominee **Natalie Wood** arrives on the red carpet in a stunning white silk gown with a halter neckline that exposes her bare back to the adoring crowd—and to her *Splendor in the Grass* costar, **Warren Beatty**, who was on the verge of superstardom. An ermine stole and evening gloves root her firmly in the past, but her beehive hairdo would soon be sported by imitators all over the country.

LUCK IN SPADES

Carroll Baker's four-leaf-clover top prefigures the boldly patterned fabrics that would become common later in the decade. She also sports the most popular look in beauty for women at the time—a strenuously back-combed crown of hair, with a thick rim of black eyeliner around her eyes. With her is **Richard Chamberlain**.

©A.M.P.A.S.®

SUCCESS STORY

Rita Moreno waltzed into the Academy Awards in a gown with a brightly patterned, full skirt and a bodice with widely cut armholes, which showed off her dancer's shoulders. Boyfriend and onscreen costar **George Chakiris** (left) was also suitably handsome in a "jet"-black tail coat, as was **Rock Hudson**.

FULL STEAM AHEAD 1963

Fashion was beginning to diversify right in front of viewers' eyes, as the Academy Awards became the backdrop against which America could watch their icons of style leave conformity behind. The gowns at this year's awards were some of the most original yet.

35TH
ACADEMY AWARDS
April 8, 1963
Santa Monica Civic Auditorium
Santa Monica
HOST: FRANK SINATRA

GIRL'S BEST FRIEND

©A.M.P.A.S.®

An aging **Joan Crawford** (with **Gregory Peck**) caused quite a stir in her flashy silver-beaded gown, tailor-made for her by costume designer Edith Head. As if the sparkling beads weren't enough, Crawford also decks herself out with enough diamonds to sink a ship. In fact, the large diamond necklace she wears (the pendant was actually a precariously attached brooch) was the same one she had worn to several ceremonies in the 1940s.

SHE'LL FLY AWAY

©A.M.P.A.S.®

Wearing what looks suspiciously like a shag rug for a collar, **Sophia Loren** presents **Gregory Peck** with the Oscar for Best Supporting Actor. Her look is much more appealing from the waist down, where her cocktail-length tulle skirt floats prettily above the stage.

GOODBYE TO ALL THAT

Former Best Actress-winner **Olivia de Havilland** (with *Lawrence of Arabia* producer **Sam Spiegel**) looks fully prepared to face the 60s in an updated take on her Oscar style—she's teased her hair, applied false eyelashes, and chosen a slim sheath, leaving the full, girlish skirts of the 50s behind. The brooch at the center of her bust lends the gown an art deco look reminiscent of the 20s.
©A.M.P.A.S.®

AND THE OSCAR® GOES TO...

Best Picture:
Lawrence of Arabia

Best Director:
David Lean,
Lawrence of Arabia

Best Actress:
Anne Bancroft,
The Miracle Worker

Best Actor:
Gregory Peck,
To Kill a Mockingbird

Best Supporting Actress:
Patty Duke,
The Miracle Worker

Best Supporting Actor:
Ed Begley,
Sweet Bird of Youth

19*64* LET FREEDOM RING

With the civil rights movement taking off, it was only fitting that Sidney Poitier won this year's Oscar for Best Actor. But that wasn't the only revolution taking place—the country's mores were quickly shifting gears, as young people clamored for more freedom in every aspect of their lives. But even though Hollywood films were beginning to portray the changes taking place across the country, the ceremony itself remained a formal affair.

36TH
ACADEMY AWARDS
April 13, 1964
Santa Monica Civic Auditorium
Santa Monica
HOST: JACK LEMMON

AND THE OSCAR® GOES TO...

Best Picture:
Tom Jones

Best Director:
Tony Richardson, *Tom Jones*

Best Actress:
Patricia Neal, *Hud*

Best Actor:
Sidney Poitier,
Lilies of the Field

Best Supporting Actress:
Margaret Rutherford,
The V.I.P.s

Best Supporting Actor:
Melvyn Douglas, *Hud*

©A.M.P.A.S.®

GETTING CHUMMY

Part Grecian goddess, part slinky screen siren, **Anne Bancroft**, who presented the Best Actor Oscar to **Sidney Poitier**, told the rising star to "enjoy it, chum, it doesn't last long." The elaborate pleats of her gown drape flatteringly over her figure, while skinny spaghetti straps keep the dress afloat. If she removed the evening gloves, she could look like a contemporary of any of today's stars in this gorgeous gown.

CHIC SHEATH

Angie Dickinson shines in this brocade sheath with matching jacket. The wide neck of the coat and the low cut of the dress frame her décolletage so well she needs no jewelry around her neck. The black evening gloves add a touch of formality and class.

LILY OF THE FIELD

In a lilac gown with Empire waist seaming that drapes to the floor, **Julie Andrews** is a perfect 10 as she presents **Federico Fellini** with his Best Foreign Language Film Oscar for *8 1/2*. She chose a Y-shaped necklace of clear beads as her jewelry for the evening.
©A.M.P.A.S.®

STYLE REVS UP 19**65**

It was nearly impossible to find a full-skirted gown at this year's ceremony, as the more hip look of the 60s really began to take hold. The decade's biggest stars arrived in sophisticated, slim-fitting gowns that recalled the subtle glamour of the 1930s—but with a funky 60s twist.

37TH
ACADEMY AWARDS
April 5, 1965
Santa Monica Civic Auditorium
Santa Monica
HOST: BOB HOPE

©A.M.P.A.S.®

AND THE OSCAR® GOES TO...

Best Picture:
My Fair Lady

Best Director:
George Cukor, *My Fair Lady*

Best Actress:
Julie Andrews, *Mary Poppins*

Best Actor:
Rex Harrison, *My Fair Lady*

Best Supporting Actress:
Lila Kedrova, *Zorba the Greek*

Best Supporting Actor:
Peter Ustinov, *Topkapi*

VANISHING POINT

Hubert de Givenchy, **Audrey Hepburn's** good friend and the only person who ever dressed her for the Oscars, designed this white satin gown. The cut of the dress, with its slight flare and high neckline, expertly hides the fact that at the time Hepburn was worrisomely underweight. But her characteristic charm and élan dazzled her colleagues and the audience enough to distract them from her figure. Elbow-length gloves and diamond-and-emerald drop earrings add the finishing, elegant touches. Also shown are **Jack Warner**, **Rex Harrison**, and **George Cukor**, all of whom were involved with the production of the film.

CULTURE CLASH

Before removing the matching silk coat from her Givenchy gown, **Audrey Hepburn** had a chat with **Jane Fonda**, who was comparatively dressed-down in a double-breasted sleeveless gown festooned with a glittering brooch. Her low-key look, which could have been worn in the daytime, was an example of the new era in Oscar dressing, in which the stars of the new vanguard no longer dressed as lavishly as their predecessors.

HEAVY METAL

A pouf is nowhere to be found on **Debbie Reynolds** in this heavily beaded, slim-fitting, floor-length sheath, as befits fashion's new silhouette. A garden's worth of beaded flowers brighten the shoulders and neck of this brilliant evening gown, while Reynolds' teased hair and heavily lined lids root the look firmly in the 60s. Standing with her are (left to right) **Andre Previn** and **Robert** and **Richard Sherman**.

©A.M.P.A.S.®

SPOTLIGHT

on Gowns: 1960s

The 1960s were like a petri dish when it came to popular culture—the era was ripe for watching radical transformations occur in all aspects of American life within the span of just a decade. The mutations that took place in the world of fashion were particularly noticeable: the first half of the decade betrayed the remnants of the prim and proper 1950s, then quickly gave way to an entirely new shift in how people presented themselves. Stars who couldn't keep up with the changes taking place were quickly relegated to the back of the fashion heap, while those who were able to adapt to changing times emerged with a fresh, new look that was as exciting as the decade.

1961

DIMPLE TIME

Annette Funicello and Shirley Temple are all smiles in gowns that clearly place them at the beginning of the decade.

Carefully curled and *controlled hairstyles* are lingering artifacts of the well-to-do 1950s.

Traditional bodices keep the women properly covered—both are form-fitting, but tastefully so. Funicello's royal blue pleats keep her appropriately contained.

The fabric on Funicello's skirt has some flash to it in the form of a metallic print, but otherwise the *full, wide skirts* of these gowns are meant to emphasize femininity and conformity—two traits that were about to go the way of the horse and buggy.

©A.M.P.A.S.®

1968
A BREAK WITH TRADITION

1969
CALLING ON COLOR

Audrey Hepburn traded in the delicate lace and powder-puff skirt she wore in 1954 and donned a radical new silhouette in 1968, designed by Givenchy, of course.

Lee Remick's gown showed that the 60s had indeed arrived and its fun new style had infiltrated the mainstream.

GIVENCHY

Not technically a gown, this two-piece ensemble features a *sparkling vest* that allows just a peek at Hepburn's navel.

ant *white bow* ties
the vest just over the
rt, lending a sweet look
to a sexy top. The bow is
corative enough to allow
burn to go without a
ecklace or other
jewelry.

est is worn
a matching
, *narrow*,
e *skirt* that
high on the
and falls to
he floor. It is
ch slimmer
the skirts
t a few
earlier, and repre-
the new tack that
shion was taking.

Flowing, *natural-like, long hair* was the norm for glamorous evening looks, replacing the overly coiffed looks of years past.

A bare, unadorned neck was in keeping with the more natural look that fashion was taking.

Purple, orange and green bands of color were drawn from the popular palette of the day.

An *unfitted, narrow gown* makes a fashionable statement—and kisses the frou-frou 50s goodbye.

Glittering paillettes at the base of the dress place this gown firmly in the funky new decade that was the 60s.

*19*66

THE HILLS ARE ALIVE

The Hollywood hills were awash in color as the Academy Awards were broadcast in Technicolor for the first time. Despite the technological achievement, the auditorium looked like a vast sea of white, as several actresses made the decision to wear the flattering color in order to show off their California tans.

38TH
ACADEMY AWARDS
April 18, 1966
Santa Monica Civic Auditorium
Santa Monica
HOST: BOB HOPE

AND THE OSCAR® GOES TO...

Best Picture:
The Sound of Music

Best Director:
Robert Wise,
The Sound of Music

Best Actress:
Julie Christie, *Darling*

Best Actor:
Lee Marvin, *Cat Ballou*

Best Supporting Actress:
Shelley Winters,
A Patch of Blue

Best Supporting Actor:
Martin Balsam,
A Thousand Clowns

©A.M.P.A.S.®

HEAD TURNER

Though past her prime, **Lana Turner** (right) still sparkles in a long-sleeved, beaded gown that clings to her curves. The high, rounded neckline was a common feature of many dresses of the 60s. With her are Kathryn Grayson, accepting the Oscar for Best Costume Designer **Phyllis Dalton**, and **James Garner**.

©A.M.P.A.S.®

MIRROR IMAGE

British newcomer and Best Actress-winner **Julie Christie** (second from left) stole the spotlight in this glittering gold jumpsuit designed by Don Bessant. The sleeveless turtleneck, belted at the waist and flowing into pants, broke the mold for Oscar-dressing—although some might say she looked a lot like another fellow made from a mold, the Oscar statue itself. Christie is shown with **Lee Marvin**, **Shelley Winters** and **Martin Balsam**.

©A.M.P.A.S.®

SLIM FAST

Lila Kedrova (shown holding the Best Supporting Actor Oscar awarded to **Martin Balsam**) wears a modified evening gown from years past—the round-necked bodice is jazzed up with glistening paillettes, while the hip-skimming satin skirt has darts sewn in to create a slimmer version of poufy skirts gone by.

STRIKE AVERTED! 1967

The star wattage was somewhat dimmer this year, as a television strike that ended just hours before the ceremony deterred many of the acting nominees from showing up. Regardless, there were still enough fashion surprises to keep the show interesting.

39TH
ACADEMY AWARDS
April 10, 1967
Santa Monica Civic Auditorium
Santa Monica
HOST: BOB HOPE

AND THE OSCAR® GOES TO...

Best Picture:
A Man for All Seasons

Best Director:
Fred Zinnemann,
A Man for All Seasons

Best Actress:
Elizabeth Taylor,
Who's Afraid of Virginia Woolf?

Best Actor:
Paul Scofield,
A Man for All Seasons

Best Supporting Actress:
Sandy Dennis,
Who's Afraid of Virginia Woolf?

Best Supporting Actor:
Walter Matthau,
The Fortune Cookie

PHOTO OP-ART

Rosemary Stack's outfit may look like it's trying to hypnotize you, but it's really just a take on one of the decade's biggest trends, the optically innovative style known as op art. The graphically bold print leads the eye every which way. With her is husband **Robert**.

©A.M.P.A.S.®

LAY, LADY, LAY

Layering was the name of the game for presenter **Candace Bergen** (far right) and **Helen Rose**, who accepted the Oscar on behalf of costume designer Irene Sharaff. Both wear gowns that came in two pieces: Bergen's featherweight cape overlays an asymmetrical sheath and ties at the shoulder in a huge bow, while Rose gets weighted down by a heavily beaded short-sleeved yoke that gives way to a filmy, pleated gown. **Anita Louise** (far left) wears a shift with beaded collar and beaded transparent sleeves. **Robert Mitchum** stands in the midst of it all.

A LITTLE LEG

Swedish actress **Inger Stevens** strikes a pose in one of the most iconic looks of the 60s—the miniskirt. Here she wears, actually, a mini-dress, but the effect is the same: viewers get a long look at the legs, which taper to a pair of heels of a very tasteful height—not so high that they look tacky, but just high enough to give the legs some shape.

19*68* GUESS WHO'S WEARING WHAT?

The outlandish fashions of the decade were becoming mainstream, but the conservative producers of the Oscars were terrified of what the stars might wear next. They implored the attendees to dress appropriately, but it was a losing battle: fashion's new wave would not be stopped.

40TH
ACADEMY AWARDS
April 10, 1968
Santa Monica Civic Auditorium
Santa Monica
HOST: BOB HOPE

AND THE OSCAR® GOES TO...

Best Picture:
In the Heat of the Night

Best Director:
Mike Nichols, *The Graduate*

Best Actress:
Katharine Hepburn, *Guess Who's Coming to Dinner*

Best Actor:
Rod Steiger, *In the Heat of the Night*

Best Supporting Actress:
Estelle Parsons, *Bonnie and Clyde*

Best Supporting Actor:
George Kennedy, *Cool Hand Luke*

©A.M.P.A.S.®

A BONNIE LASS

The gorgeous **Faye Dunaway**, hoping for a Best Actress win for her role in *Bonnie and Clyde*, arrived at the awards show in an unconventional black satin dress designed by Theadora Van Runkle bedecked with silk flowers and a train. Offscreen, the outfits Dunaway's Bonnie character wore onscreen sparked a hugely popular street trend called the "Bonnie look," distinguished by the juxtaposition of beret, neckerchief, knee-length skirts and stockings.

GRADUATED SHIFT

The mark of the 60s is all over **Leslie Caron's** unfitted shift dress. The cutaway armholes and high, round neckline trimmed with beads and sequins were new features in evening dressing. The crepe dress culminates in a chevron of beads, sequins and large paillettes that dangle engagingly above the hem of the dress. (Shown with **Mike Nichols**.)

CHER-ING THE LOVE

Sonny Bono's damask Cossack suit and **Cher's** cotton candy stripes and braids helped spread free love at the Academy Awards. This is probably the most covered up Cher has ever been at the Oscars.

ALL GROWN UP

Patty Duke finally looks her age in this sexy shirt-dress that is open to just above her rhinestone-encrusted belt. The wide collar, long, fitted sleeves and belted waist were harbingers of the immensely popular wrapdresses that would emerge in the 1970s.

©A.M.P.A.S.®

WORLDWIDE EXPOSURE 1969

The powers that be finally relented and relaxed their restrictions on the dress code for this year's show. Meanwhile, the awards were being broadcast to a record 37 countries around the world, inspiring, perhaps, some stars to don their most outrageous outfits yet. Without a doubt, this was the year the Oscars received the greatest exposure—as did some of its stars.

41ST
ACADEMY AWARDS
April 14, 1969
Dorothy Chandler Pavilion
Los Angeles Music Center
Los Angeles
HOST: "FRIENDS
OF OSCAR"

AND THE OSCAR® GOES TO...

Best Picture:
Oliver!

Best Director:
Carol Reed, *Oliver!*

Best Actress:
Katharine Hepburn,
The Lion in Winter and
Barbra Streisand, *Funny Girl*

Best Actor:
Cliff Robertson, *Charly*

Best Supporting Actress:
Ruth Gordon,
Rosemary's Baby

Best Supporting Actor:
Jack Albertson,
The Subject Was Roses

IF YOU'RE GOING TO SAN FRANCISCO ...

Best Actress-nominee **Vanessa Redgrave** arrives at the Academy Awards with flowers in her hair. Her ethnic-inspired robe is worn over a more traditional-looking silk gown. Her date, Italian actor **Franco Nero**, wears a dress shirt made of lace eyelets all up the way up to his stand-up collar.

©A.M.P.A.S.®

"HELLO, GORGEOUS!"

Barbra Streisand's see-through Arnold Scaasi pajamas marked a sea change in Oscar fashion. Once Hollywood and the crowd at home got a glimpse of Babs' buns through that sheer fabric, the fashion cat was out of the bag forever. The Peter Pan collar on this outfit is totally incongruous with the black, sequined, bell-bottomed pajama bottoms, paving the way for another new Oscar trend: incomprehensible taste.

©A.M.P.A.S.®

BACKGROUND BEAUTIES

Natalie Wood (center) and **Jane Fonda** (right) graciously share the limelight with **L. Ludmilla Saveyeva**, who accepted the Oscar for Best Foreign Film, *War and Peace.* Wood looks on in a brightly colored print dress, with perhaps the Academy Award's first exposed nipple, while Fonda is more covered in a bell-sleeved, sheer, beaded gown with fringe at the sleeves.

THE BIG WHITE DRESS

Ever since Coco Chanel introduced the little black dress, no well-dressed woman has been seen at a cocktail party without one. But "little" and "black" (read, "subdued") are two words that don't belong in any Hollywood diva's vocabulary. For the vampiest, most glamorous effect a screen siren can summon, she turns to her secret weapon: the big white dress. White reflects klieg lights, shows off California tans, and looks especially good on blondes. So of course a white dress, preferably a low-cut, floor-length number in luminescent satin, is a natural choice for any heat-seeking starlet—hence this gallery of the big white dress in all its incarnations through the years.

1974

1996

Dyan Cannon's big white dress is cut down to there, and shows plenty of suntanned cleavage. She opted to dress this glamorous gown down by wearing giant silver cuffs on each wrist and a daisy in her hair.

Courtney Love shocked everyone when the former grunge rocker turned up at the Awards in a stunning white silk Versace gown and platinum hair. Her gown, hair and Harry Winston diamonds brought a touch of old Hollywood glamour to the Awards.

1998

In a white jersey Richard Tyler gown slit up to the top of her thigh, **Ashley Judd** made grown men cry when she strutted onto the Academy stage in 1998. Perhaps fearing that her uber-sexy look would be too much to take, she feigned innocence by putting pretty white gardenias in her hair.

1993

Supermodel **Cindy Crawford** was stunning in this not-so-big white dress. With her is **Richard Gere**.

1961

1956

A Greco-Romanesque twist at the neck and a brocade bodice show **Peggy Connolly** (with **Frank Sinatra**) dressing her way.

Skinny spaghetti straps and elaborate pleats that tuck under themselves create a look that helps **Tina Louise** show off her assets to the greatest effect.

THE 1970s

THE AGE OF AQUARIUS ...

A spirit of sexy eclecticism permeated the 70s, an era in which bad taste was good taste, and the more eclectic the outfit, the better. The "me decade" ushered a slew of irreverent new looks onto the red carpet, as style increasingly became a matter of individual taste. Nowhere was this better represented than in Hollywood, where actors had the money and access to designers who could tailor outfits to the stars' distinct (and sometimes outrageous) tastes. Ironically, it was the hippies, the very antithesis of Hollywood glamour, who made individuality the mark of 70s fashion and embraced the free-spirit ethos in which, truly, anything went

FASHION ON FILM

Annie Hall (1977)

Diane Keaton—with a little help from Ralph Lauren, who designed many of the outfits for this film—made menswear chic in her baggy trousers, vests and ties. American women immediately embraced the style, which was both easy to wear and decidedly hip, and the Annie Hall look became a signature of the 70s.

A Star is Born (1976)

Starring as vagabond musicians, Kris Kristofferson and Barbra Streisand showcased the 1970s fashion aesthetic— for better or worse. Though seen almost as kitsch in retrospect, the outfits displayed a range of hippie styles, all with a rock'n'roll edge. Barbra's over-the-top wardrobe was credited in the film to "her closet".

DESIGNERS TO THE STARS: 1970s

HALSTON (1932–1990)

Jet Set Darling

It's hard to think of Roy Halston Frowick without thinking of the celebrities who frequented Studio 54 in the 1970s wearing his clothes. Halston, as he was known, made silk jersey one of the most popular clothing fabrics in the 70s. His clothes for day were sleek and minimalist, while his evening clothes were sexy, glamorous and cut close to the body—the perfect complement to Hollywood's body-conscious starlets. His pared down clothes were well-suited to celebrities and their jet-set lifestyles, and as a result he became one of the most celebrated designers of the decadent decade. He was frequently photographed outside the notorious Studio 54 with clients like Liza Minnelli and Elizabeth Taylor.

VALENTINO (1932–)

Evening Star

Valentino Garavani designed flamboyant, romantic evening gowns that often outshone the stars themselves. Luminaries such as Jackie Onassis and Elizabeth Taylor were fans of the designer's extravagant creations, and showed them off to great effect. Valentino's trademark color was a vivid orange-red, which he used repeatedly in his designs, endearing him to ostentatious celebrities everywhere.

PIERRE CARDIN (1922–)

An Ever-Evolving Style

The innovative use of new, supple fabrics and a propensity for sun-ray pleating helped Pierre Cardin catch the eye of Hollywood's elite. He became affiliated with film when he designed the costumes for Jean Cocteau's *La Belle et la bête* in 1946. He also achieved widespread recognition for his Space Age designs in the 60s. By the 70s, he had turned to more traditional, yet still inventive, dressmaking techniques. For big nights out, the brightest stars of the day luxuriated in the designer's exquisite layered chiffon evening gowns.

PIERRE CARDI

19*70* IN BLOOM

The decade started off swinging with stars dressed to show off their true, albeit gussied-up, selves. Although the really outrageous outfits wouldn't enter the stage for a few years, the break with traditional Oscar-night dressing was already palpable. 70s fashion was blooming—it just wasn't yet in full flower.

AND THE OSCAR® GOES TO...

Best Picture:
Midnight Cowboy

Best Director:
John Schlesinger,
Midnight Cowboy

Best Actress:
Maggie Smith,
The Prime of Miss Jean Brodie

Best Actor:
John Wayne,
True Grit

Best Supporting Actress:
Goldie Hawn,
Cactus Flower

Best Supporting Actor:
Gig Young,
They Shoot Horses, Don't They?

FASHION FORWARD

Always ahead of her time, **Liza Minnelli** (escorted down the red carpet by her film-director father, **Vincente Minnelli**) is a standout in a deeply cut halter dress and wide choker. The slinky look of this gown would soon become a mainstay of 70s fashion for the jet set, but Minnelli had it wrapped-up first.

PRINCESS BRIDE

Raquel Welch (collecting the Best Supporting Actress award on behalf of Goldie Hawn for Hawn's role in *Cactus Flower*) looks something like a flower herself in this elaborately decorated frock. A patchwork of colors, fabrics and designs, and featuring an empire waist, this dress has a vaguely medieval feel that clashed with Welch's modern sexpot reputation. **Gig Young** wears a more traditional tux.

©A.M.P.A.S.®

PRETTY IN PINK

Barbra Streisand, in a pink dress with matching pillbox hat, gets cozy with **John Wayne**.

©A.M.P.A.S.®

LOVE STORY

Ali McGraw shares a laugh with husband **Bob Evans** as they enter the awards show. McGraw wears a two-toned cap and fringed shawl over her baroque-patterned dress.

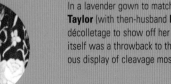

INDIGO ICE

In a lavender gown to match her famously violet eyes, **Elizabeth Taylor** (with then-husband **Richard Burton**) finds the perfect décolletage to show off her 69-carat diamond necklace. The gown itself was a throwback to the prim and proper 50s, but the generous display of cleavage most certainly was not.

19*71* FLORAL PRINCESSES

43RD
ACADEMY AWARDS
April 15, 1971
Dorothy Chandler Pavilion
Los Angeles
HOSTS:
THE YEAR'S NOMINEES

Several nominees stayed home this year, but there was still plenty of fashion excitement to be found on the red carpet. From old-school floral prints to flowers in the hair, 1971 showed just how colorful the decade could be.

AND THE OSCAR® GOES TO...

Best Picture:
Patton

Best Director:
Franklin J. Schaffner,
Patton

Best Actress:
Glenda Jackson,
Women in Love

Best Actor:
George C. Scott,
Patton

Best Supporting Actress:
Helen Hayes,
Airport

Best Supporting Actor:
John Mills,
Ryan's Daughter

FLOWER GIRL

With a flower planted squarely on her head and a floral-trimmed décolletage, **Goldie Hawn** upgrades the icons of the 60s in this fun and funky Oscar gown. Her dress may be 70s casual, but her heavily lined eyes and false eyelashes are leftovers from the 60s.

SIMPLY PRETTY

Accepting the Irving Thalberg award on behalf of her lover, Ingmar Bergman, **Liv Ullmann** wears a simple gown featuring a sheer floral print and wide, fluttering sleeves. Her simple strand of pearls and neatly coiffed hairdo lend her a pretty, subtle look unlikely to steal the limelight from her sexier counterparts.

RATHER REVEALING

Sally Kellerman foreshadows the braless, see-through look that Jennifer Lopez would make her own 30 years later. Kellerman's husband, **Rick Edelstein**, escorts her.

TIME TRAVELERS

Love Story author **Erich Segal** and actress **Jane Alexander** look like visitors from another epoch in their Oscar-night outfits. Her curled hair and brocade-trimmed gown with balloon sleeves and his smoking jacket make them appear as if they've just emerged from a parlor visit.

FLOWER POWER

Ali McGraw gives a nod to the hippie movement in this crocheted cap in shades of lilac, pink and purple. Her stick-straight, shiny hair would become a staple of beauty for the rest of the decade.

CARRYIN' ON

Leslie Caron holds her Oscar high in a floral-print gown with ruched sleeves and handkerchief hems.

1972 FREE AS A BIRD

You could hardly pin down one single fashion trend at this year's Oscars, as the stars were wearing just about everything under the rainbow. From up-to-the-minute and sexy to sweet and old-fashioned, everyone found something to suit their own individual tastes.

44TH
ACADEMY AWARDS
April 10, 1972
Dorothy Chandler Pavilion
Los Angeles
HOSTS: VARIOUS

AND THE OSCAR® GOES TO...

Best Picture:
The French Connection

Best Director:
William Friedkin,
The French Connection

Best Actress:
Jane Fonda,
Klute

Best Actor:
Gene Hackman,
The French Connection

Best Supporting Actress:
Cloris Leachman,
The Last Picture Show

Best Supporting Actor:
Ben Johnson,
The Last Picture Show

A CASUAL AIR

Best Supporting Actress **Cloris Leachman** is a natural beauty with her straight, parted-down-the-middle hair and low-cut sundress with a bloused bodice. As if that weren't casual enough, there isn't a drop of jewelry to be found anywhere on her—the only glitter comes from the little gold guy she holds in her hands.
©A.M.P.A.S.®

OLD AS NEW

Arriving to pick up his Best Actor Oscar (although he doesn't yet know it), **Gene Hackman** and wife **Fay** make an offbeat pair. She chose an old-fashioned gown with a high neck and a transparent yoke embroidered with a flowery detail—a popular style with brides at the time.

©A.M.P.A.S.®

WE'RE FONDA JANE!

The G.I.'s returning from Vietnam might not have agreed, but plenty of people thought **Jane Fonda's** *Klute* shag was cute. Lopping off her lustrous locks was a brave move for an actress prized for her looks, and her edgy haircut sparked imitations in liberated women everywhere. She and **Gene Hackman** enjoyed their Oscars, won for Best Supporting Actress and Actor.

21?

Connie Stevens looks more like playing cards on a black-jack table than an actress in this spectacularly busy gown in shades of black, red, yellow and blue.

HOLLYWOOD ROYALTY

Ann-Margret (with **Roger Smith**) looks regal in a royal blue, Asian-influenced gown festooned with a natural-looking motif of vines and flowers. The white fur coat worn over it adds to the glamorous aura.

1973

A FAMILY AFFAIR

As the outfits of some stars became increasingly outrageous, more conservative dressers got stiffer, more traditional and more covered up—perhaps in a metaphorical upturned nose to the "me" generation and its impropriety.

45TH
ACADEMY AWARDS
March 27, 1973
Dorothy Chandler Pavilion
Los Angeles
HOSTS: VARIOUS

AND THE OSCAR® GOES TO...

Best Picture:
The Godfather

Best Director:
Bob Fosse,
Cabaret

Best Actress:
Liza Minnelli,
Cabaret

Best Actor:
Marlon Brando,
The Godfather

Best Supporting Actress:
Eileen Heckart,
Butterflies Are Free

Best Supporting Actor:
Joel Grey,
Cabaret

HI, MOM!

©A.M.P.A.S.®

Best Supporting Actress-winner **Eileen Heckart** poses in an unusual two-toned gown with an asymmetrical slash of color that drapes over her right arm. She was reported to have said that she hoped the TV camera would pan on her so that her mother in Ohio could see the dress. The previous year's Best Supporting Actress winner, **Cloris Leachman**, presented the Oscar in a gown much flashier than the one she wore when she accepted her own Oscar.

GLITTERING VINES

Liv Ullmann wears a close-fitting gown with a psychedelic print, overlaid with a creeping vine of sparkles. This is a look that pays lip service to the wild things happening in fashion without going all the way—the gown is really a rather conservative number that only nods at the 70s' madcap styles.

ALL IN THE FAMILY

Best Picture-director **Francis Ford Coppola** holds his Oscar while **Dorothy Puzo**, daughter of Mario Puzo, holds the award for Best Adapted Screenplay her father received for his work translating his book *The Godfather* into a film. In a uniquely hippie-style gown of loose fabric and flowers, she is practically a poster child for the free-form looks of the 1970s.

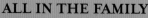

©A.m.p.a.s.®

SHE'S NO ANGEL

A simple strand of beads around her neck and a sporty patterned gown set off **Kate Jackson's** dark hair.

HOLLYWOOD RUFFLE

Connie Kreski (with **James Caan**) blends 70s natural good looks with the sort of modish gown that was influenced by the street fashions of London in the 60s. Her ruffled, multicolored gown is both sexy and fun.

COWBOYS AND INDIANS

The Far East meets the Wild West in **Dyan Cannon's** bizarre stylized suit, which she accessorized with a bindi on her forehead.

HOT NIGHT, WARM FUR

James Brolin and then-wife **Jane** stand outside the theater in clothes adopted from the mods and the hippies: his tie defies the conventional styles, and her patchwork coat features a giant fur collar.

*19*74 THE NAKED TRUTH

Whatever else might have been happening in fashion, there is one Oscar attendee who will forever be remembered for precisely what he didn't wear: Streaker Robert Opal, the proprietor of a San Francisco sex shop, stunned the audience and presenters by running across the stage on live TV in nothing but his birthday suit—perhaps the ultimate expression of 1970s sartorial instincts.

46TH
ACADEMY AWARDS
April 2, 1974
Dorothy Chandler Pavilion
Los Angeles
HOSTS: VARIOUS

AND THE OSCAR® GOES TO...

Best Picture:
The Sting

Best Director:
George Roy Hill,
The Sting

Best Actress:
Glenda Jackson,
A Touch of Class

Best Actor:
Jack Lemmon,
Save the Tiger

Best Supporting Actress:
Tatum O'Neal,
Paper Moon

Best Supporting Actor:
John Houseman,
The Paper Chase

CLOGS 'N TOGS

The iconoclastic **Katharine Hepburn** put on no airs for her first Oscar appearance—in fact, she barely got dressed. It was rumored she went straight from working in her garden to the ceremony, in her clogs and gardening clothes.

BEACH BUNS

Cher left little to the imagination when she donned this outfit, more suitable for a Hawaiian luau than an awards ceremony.

CLOAKED LADY

Paula Prentiss (with **Richard Benjamin**) exudes laid-back 70s sex appeal in this fringed and embroidered tunic with a cotton cloak on top. Her thick, tousled hair furthers the easygoing vibe, but note her metallic mesh evening bag: it gives her hippie style a touch of disco flash.

STICK FIGURE

One of the world's first super-models, the English beauty **Twiggy**, waits to present the Oscar for Best Costume Design to Edith Head. Her peasant-style gown was clearly influenced by the hippie movement then taking place.

SCREEN SIREN

Raquel Welch is the epitome of the 70s sexpot in this pale peach beaded halter top that ties with a heavily fringed sash at the waist. Her beaded choker and full, wavy hair give her a contradictory glammed-up look—which suited the confusing era perfectly.

*19*75 RAINDROPS KEEP FALLING

Torrential downpours and a soggy red carpet did nothing to dampen the spirits of the stars at this year's awards. With little care for anyone else's ideas of what "fashion" was about, they arrived in psychedelic swirls of color and flowing gowns, putting their personal stamps on whatever they chose to wear.

47TH
ACADEMY AWARDS
April 8, 1975
Dorothy Chandler Pavilion
Los Angeles
HOSTS: VARIOUS

AND THE OSCAR® GOES TO...

Best Picture:
The Godfather, Part II

Best Director:
Francis Ford Coppola,
The Godfather, Part II

Best Actress:
Ellen Burstyn,
Alice Doesn't Live Here Anymore

Best Actor:
Art Carney,
Harry and Tonto

Best Supporting Actress:
Ingrid Bergman,
Murder on the Orient Express

Best Supporting Actor:
Robert De Niro,
The Godfather: Part II

SATIN DOLLS

Michael Douglas and **Brenda Vaccaro** gleam as they arrive at the Academy Awards. Vaccaro's sexy gown features a deep neckline, fitted bodice panel and double spaghetti straps embellished with jewels.

HERE'S LOOKIN' AT HER

Screen-legend **Ingrid Bergman** stands regally with her Oscar in a loose, pale turquoise gown printed with flowers. With this outfit, the aging beauty found a way to embrace the spirit of the eclectic 70s without succumbing to an undignified look.

©A.M.P.A.S.®

BOMBSHELL BACALL

The ever-glamorous **Lauren Bacall** is ravishing in a black floor-length gown with a plunging neckline—in stark contrast to **Theoni Aldrich**, who stands next to her in a much less revealing, menswear-influenced ensemble.

©A.M.P.A.S.®

GRADUATION NIGHT

Katharine Ross, with an unidentified companion, arrives in a beautifully draped sea-green gown that accentuates her gorgeous figure. The straps that fall over her shoulders and the sash at her waist evoke images of a Grecian goddess.

BLURRING THE LINES

Cher muddies up her fashion cues and arrives at the Oscars in a gown of indeterminate color and style—she looks more like a mud puddle than an actress.

WEATHERING THE STORM

Despite the rain, **Jack Nicholson** showed up in sunglasses, beret and full tuxedo. Long-term love **Anjelica Huston** pairs a sleek, sequined gown and soft, straight hair to dazzling effect—she radiates subtle 70s sexiness.

CLIFFHANGER

Raquel Welch (with **Jon Voight**) sizzles in this strapless gown that accentuates the actress's ample figure.

87

SPOTLIGHT
on Gowns: EARLY 1970s

RAQUEL WELCH

**RAQUEL PLAYS THE PART
OF A MEDIEVAL PRINCESS**

Raquel Welch's ensemble was like nothing anyone had seen before at the Oscars. She blended the ethnic influences of the 60s with the muted colors of the 70s to create something entirely new in formalwear.

Raquel *curled her long hair*, pinned it up at the sides, then let if fall naturally to her shoulders and décolletage.

This was perhaps the most colorful gown yet worn to the Oscars—muted *pinks, mauves, yellows and greens* blended together in an ode to the natural look that was prevalent in the 70s.

A *rope tie* at the waist g
form to Welch's figure in
casual manner.

The *bell-shaped* sleeve was a new look in fashion for the Oscars. Again, the shape of the dress recalled the nature-inspired clothes that were fashionable in the 70s.

LIZA MINNELLI
MINNELLI GOES MINIMAL

Compared to Raquel Welch, Liza Minnelli's sexy, minimalist halter-neck gown showed the opposite end of the spectrum of 70s dressing.

Minnelli's hair is *short and sassy*, a foil to the overt sexiness of the gown.

Her *thick choker* draws attention to her face and breaks the line between her neck and décolletage, putting more of the spotlight on the gown.

The *plunging neckline* shows just enough cleavage to be stylishly provocative.

As was the style in the 70s, Minnelli's gown *hugs the body* and falls straight to the floor, emphasizing slim hips and a slender figure

ELIZABETH TAYLOR
LIZ DRESSES DOWN

Even the usually glamorous Elizabeth Taylor took a cue from her more casual colleagues and dressed down during the natural 70s. It was a look that was short-lived for the diva, who attended later Oscar ceremonies in full movie-star regalia.

Taylor keeps her hair relatively *loose and flowing*, pinning it up only at the back and sides.

Her *neckline is plunging but bare*, as Taylor opted not to dress it up with diamonds, in keeping with the more informal flair of her floral gown.

Taylor's gown features *short sleeves with ruffles*, an informal style more suited to daywear than an evening gown.

Taylor was sure to show off her small waist—no matter how casual the gown, she was unlikely to pass up an opportunity to *flaunt her figure*.

1976

STYLES GONE WILD

In the true high-low style that was equal parts 70s flash and campy kitsch, Lily Tomlin wore a cheap tiara to the Oscars—a parody of the vanishing glamour of previous ceremonies. But while some celebrities were mixing up their styles with an eye toward the lighthearted, there was still plenty of serious dressing going on.

48TH
ACADEMY AWARDS
March 29, 1976
Dorothy Chandler Pavilion
Los Angeles
HOSTS: VARIOUS

AND THE OSCAR® GOES TO...

Best Picture:
One Flew Over the Cuckoo's Nest

Best Director:
Milos Forman,
One Flew Over the Cuckoo's Nest

Best Actress:
Louise Fletcher,
One Flew Over the Cuckoo's Nest

Best Actor:
Jack Nicholson,
One Flew Over the Cuckoo's Nest

Best Supporting Actress:
Lee Grant,
Shampoo

Best Supporting Actor:
George Burns,
The Sunshine Boys

©A.M.P.A.S.®

WITH THIS OSCAR ... I THEE WED?
Lee Grant walked down the aisle in a used wedding dress to pick up her Best Supporting Actress Oscar. The lace details, pintucks, and tiny pompoms on the dress are prime examples of the sweet, country look that was one of many fashion statements in the 70s.

CROWNING GLORY
Lily Tomlin strides into the Oscars dressed like the screen queens of eras gone by ... sort of. Her tongue-in-cheek getup was hard to take seriously. With her is **John G. Avildsen**.

RAVISHING IN RED
All eyes were on **Elizabeth Taylor** as she took center stage in this strapless gown by Halston. Tying at the bosom and draping to the floor, this ravishing gown is one of the most gorgeous Oscar has ever seen. The color was christened, "Elizabeth Taylor Red" by the designer.

NO NURSE RATCHED
Best Actress-winner **Louise Fletcher** looks a far cry from her performance as a nightmarish nurse in *One Flew Over the Cuckoo's Nest* in this angelic sheer ensemble. She gave her acceptance speech in sign language so that her deaf parents could understand her.

LOWER AND LOWER

Marlo Thomas's plunging halter neck gown, with a bow tied at the waist, is a dazzling example of sexy 1970s styling. Escorting the lovely lady is Rod McKuen.

HEMINGWAY'S HEMLINES

Ernest Hemingway's granddaughter **Margaux Hemingway**, is draped in cabana-style stripes. The wide, diagonal stripes and halter top give the gown a beachy, breezy, yet glamorous feel.

CAPED CRUSADER

A striped cape slung over one shoulder lends **Jacqueline Bisset** a superhero Oscar look. She gazes out at the audience with a pout that's stronger than Kryptonite.

HOLDING HER BREATH?

Goldie Hawn turns blue for this year's Oscars in a beaded and fringed flapper-style gown, updated by her trademark golden corkscrew curls and a black fur stole.

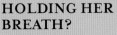

1977 PUNCH DRUNK

49TH
ACADEMY AWARDS
March 28, 1977
Dorothy Chandler Pavilion
Los Angeles
HOSTS: VARIOUS

Finally, even the show's producer had to admit it: people were more interested in watching the Oscars to see what people were wearing than to find out who won. The stars seemed to have caught on, too, and were more than willing to give the fans at home the fashion show they craved.

AND THE OSCAR® GOES TO...

Best Picture:
Rocky

Best Director:
John G. Avildsen,
Rocky

Best Actress:
Faye Dunaway,
Network

Best Actor:
Peter Finch,
Network

Best Supporting Actress:
Beatrice Straight,
Network

Best Supporting Actor:
Jason Robards,
All the President's Men

©A.M.P.A.S.®

FAYE'S DUNAWAY WITH STRUCTURE
Adopting a feature seen in many 1970s gowns, **Faye Dunaway's** dress is cinched at the waist with a tasseled rope tie, lending a more natural, "undone" look to the black silk gown.

STRAIGHT-UP GLAMOUR
In her sheer sash and overlay, **Beatrice Straight** brings a little old-time glamour to the red carpet. The accordion pleated skirt and long, draped sash add the finishing touches to this stately gown.

PLEATS, PLEASE!
The first Oscar-winning actress to also win an award for music (she cowrote the song "Evergreen" with **Paul Williams**, also pictured), **Barbra Streisand** squeezed herself into accordion pleats to accept her Oscar. A master of transformation, Ms. Streisand showed up at each awards show looking completely different, hairstyle and all.

©A.M.P.A.S.®

POSTHUMOUS HONOR

Peter Finch's glamorous widow **Eletha Finch** (with **Faye Dunaway** and an unidentified escort) accepts her husband's posthumous award for Best Actor in a mink coat and strand of pearls. Here she shows what she had on underneath: a sophisticated black sheath.

©A.M.P.A.S.®

YIN AND YANG

Jane Alexander matches her date with a black lace-top gown with contrasting white satin skirt and a feathery, white wrap.

CLOSET RAIDERS

Lee Grant upgraded from last year's choice of a vintage wedding dress, donning instead this much dressier black and blue gown. Meanwhile, **Cicely Tyson** took a cue from her companion's previous choice and wears a white lace eyelet gown, fancifully accessorized with a pink flower choker.

OFF THE CUFF

Dyan Cannon (with daughter Jennifer) wears a casually sexy off-the-shoulder knit gown that combines the two main trends of the 70s: the natural, hippie style and sexy glamour.

1978

MELLOW YELLOW

It was a year of very, very casual outfits, perhaps best epitomized by Diane Keaton's low-key *Annie Hall* look. Other stars chose casual gowns or outlandish outfits.

50TH
ACADEMY AWARDS
April 3, 1978
Dorothy Chandler Pavilion
Los Angeles
HOST: BOB HOPE

AND THE OSCAR® GOES TO...

Best Picture:
Annie Hall

Best Director:
Woody Allen,
Annie Hall

Best Actress:
Diane Keaton,
Annie Hall

Best Actor:
Richard Dreyfuss,
The Goodbye Girl

Best Supporting Actress:
Vanessa Redgrave,
Julia

Best Supporting Actor:
Jason Robards,
Julia

©A.M.P.A.S.®

DIVINE PRESENCE

Looking a bit more like a monk than a Best Supporting Actress Winner, **Vanessa Redgrave** took the stage in a bell-sleeved, medieval looking getup with tiny bows at each end of the off-the-shoulder neckline. Her pageboy haircut and lack of jewelry complete the ascetic look.

FAWCETT POURS IT ON

Farrah Fawcett wears a sporty, sexy gold lamé mini-dress that dares to bare a lot. With her famously feathered hair, heavily lined eyes and sparkling gown, she doesn't need any jewelry to accentuate her outfit.

OH, BOY

Diane Keaton won the Oscar for Best Actress, but she could have easily won an award for Best Trendsetter while she was at it. Her character in *Annie Hall* changed all the rules about how women dressed, and Keaton kept the look alive even off the set. She shares a moment with Best Actor-winner **Richard Dreyfuss**.

©A.M.P.A.S.®

STAR WARS VICTORS

Marcia Lucas, wife of *Star Wars* director **George Lucas** (pictured) carries the Oscar she won for best achievement in film editing for her husband's film. She looks anything but spacy in a gigantic fur coat and shimmering gown.

©A.M.P.A.S.®

KEY TO HER HEART

Jane Powell glows in the spotlight in a white gown with a keyhole bodice and matching gilded purse.

©A.M.P.A.S.®

IT'S A WRAP

Goldie Hawn sports one of the wrap dresses that were incredibly popular in the 70s, thanks to designer Diane Von Furstenberg. This is an evening update on the iconic style, with a deep décolletage and a high slit on the thigh. With her is **Jon Voight**.

BOUND FOR XANADU

The pantsuit gets an update: **Olivia Newton-John** wears a sheer gown over a satin pantsuit that might well have previously been worn dancing the night away at a disco.

1979 THE PARTY'S OVER

The decade was nearing its end, about to give way to a less experimental time—the 80s. But the 70s still had one last hurrah, and the stars shone in a few knockout ensembles before bidding the era goodbye.

51ST
ACADEMY AWARDS
April 9, 1979
Dorothy Chandler Pavilion
Los Angeles
HOST: JOHNNY CARSON

AND THE OSCAR® GOES TO...

Best Picture:
The Deer Hunter

Best Director:
Michael Cimino,
The Deer Hunter

Best Actress:
Jane Fonda,
Coming Home

Best Actor:
Jon Voight,
Coming Home

Best Supporting Actress:
Maggie Smith,
California Suite

Best Supporting Actor:
Christopher Walken,
The Deer Hunter

©A.M.P.A.S.®

LOOSE CANNON
Best Supporting Actress-nominee **Dyan Cannon** takes the arm of Best Supporting Actor-winner **Christopher Walken** in a columnar gown with draped front panel and a strikingly original necklace. Note, too, her heavily feathered hair—Farrah Fawcett wasn't the only one to have a lock on the style she inspired.

SLINKY SIREN
Kim Novak works it in a drop-dead sexy dress that emphasizes every curve. The giant brooch in the center of the gown gives the look an old-fashioned seductiveness.

©A.M.P.A.S.®

HAIR AGAIN
Best Actress-winner **Jane Fonda** exults in her victory. Her *Klute* shag has transformed into Fawcett-style waves, the fitting complement to a loose, printed dress sprinkled with paillettes.
©A.M.P.A.S.®

BLUE LAGOON

Carol Lynley ratchets up the fashion meter in this brilliant aqua strapless gown, which features a high slit and gathered bodice.

CHOKED UP

Raquel Welch's royal blue sequined cat suit is so tight it's a wonder she can breathe. Even her neck has been squeezed into a gold choker.

RED ALERT

This red silk gown falls gracefully around the legendary **Lauren Bacall**, who stands with Oscar-winner **Oliver Stone** (Best Screenplay). The gown is tied at the waist with a golden sash that matches Bacall's golden mane.

©A.M.P.A.S.®

NOT JOKING AROUND

A bloused, strapless white gown with a slit up the side gives **Margot Kidder** a sweet yet sexy appeal. The flowers in her hair and white scarf around her neck soften the look.

MENSWEAR

Whether it's fair or not, men tend to get short shrift at the Academy Awards. Women soak up all the attention, while the guys on their arms get passed over by the fashion brigade. But every now and then a male attendee will go out of his way to make a statement on the red carpet. Sometimes he draws attention by donning an elegant traditional tuxedo. Other times it's by breaking all the rules: A colored scarf here, a tie left in the closet at home, a pair of sunglasses and voila!—men get their chance to stand out in a sea of black.

©A.M.P.A.S.®

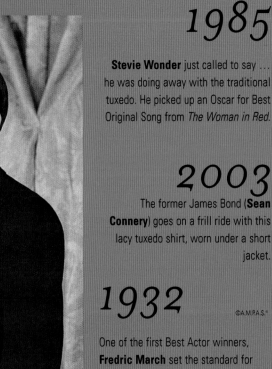

1985

Stevie Wonder just called to say … he was doing away with the traditional tuxedo. He picked up an Oscar for Best Original Song from *The Woman in Red*.

2003

The former James Bond (**Sean Connery**) goes on a frill ride with this lacy tuxedo shirt, worn under a short jacket.

1932

©A.M.P.A.S.®

One of the first Best Actor winners, **Fredric March** set the standard for Oscar-night dressing in this traditional full-dress tuxedo, complete with tails and notched lapels.

1990

Spike Lee jazzed up his tux with a colorful kente cloth scarf from Kenya. His film *Do the Right Thing* was nominated for Best Screenplay.

1988

Not content to just put his best face forward, **Chevy Chase** showed us what he wore underneath his tuxedo (whether we wanted to see it or not).

1978

Sylvester Stallone punches-up evening wear by leaving his tie at home. The open collar of his shirt offered everyone at home a peek at his hairy chest and solidified his tough-guy persona.

1977

With wife **Jan** in a wine-colored gown, **Mickey Rooney** gets groovy in a powder-blue tuxedo with contrasting trim on the lapels and pockets, plus a big, floppy bow tie.

1943

Producer **David O. Selznick** went straight and narrow in a pin-striped suit he could have worn to the office earlier that day. He escorts **Ingrid Bergman** into the ceremony.

1980s

A MATERIAL WORLD

The 1980s turned its back on the yellow smiley faces of the 70s and switched its focus to something a little greener: the mighty dollar. The economy was booming and people were suddenly more interested in making money than making "love, not war." Unbridled consumerism replaced political activism as the pastime of choice, and people were more focused on their careers than ever before. The object of the game was to make money, then show the world that you had it. "Dress for success" was everybody's mantra, especially women, who were entering the business world in droves for the first time. In order to ease the transition to a man's world, the fashion for women became increasingly masculine. Giant shoulder pads were de rigueur for any woman who wished to be taken seriously, and were often worn under jackets with a straight, slim skirt. The look of moneyed indulgence was captured in nighttime soap operas like *Dallas* and *Dynasty* and in the fashion-conscious cop show *Miami Vice*. Of course, the extravagant, excessive styles of the 80s were tailor-made for Hollywood, and celebrities relished the chance to go to the Oscars in the showiest of ostentatious gowns. Though they often erred on the side of vulgarity, the stars had to be forgiven: they were merely dedicated followers of fashion, and subtlety was not a part of the fashion scene during the decade of excess.

Top Gun (1986)

Tom Cruise made aviator sunglasses cool, and costar Kelly McGillis made bomber jackets sexy. The pair sizzled onscreen, and offscreen the whole country was copying their California-cool look.

Desperately Seeking Susan (1985)

Madonna was singing about being a virgin and a material girl, but her style could best be observed in her hit film Desperately Seeking Susan. Madonna's first fashion incarnation made parachute pants, fingerless lace gloves, black rubber bracelets and permed hair must-haves for every American teenager.

DESIGNERS TO THE STARS: 1980s

GIORGIO ARMANI (1934–)

A Master Tailer

Italian designer Giorgio Armani designed exquisitely tailored clothes that matched the 80s penchant for sharp dressing. Having created the costumes for Richard Gere's star-making turn in *American Gigolo* at the beginning of the decade, he was a natural choice for Hollywood when it came time to dress for the Oscars. Armani appealed to men, and designed tuxedos for Mel Gibson, Robin Williams and Denzel Washington, but with the power-dressing trend for women gaining popularity, actresses soon began donning his duds, too. He remains one of the most popular designers in Hollywood on Oscar night, and has dressed nearly every power player in Tinseltown, from top studio executives to top stars like Michelle Pfeiffer, Julia Roberts and Jodie Foster.

CHRISTIAN LACROIX (1951–)

Lavish and Luxurious

At the opposite end of the spectrum from the cool, refined designs of Armani lie the styles of Christian Lacroix, the Paris couturier who epitomized the unrestrained, over-the-top look of the 80s. His balloon skirt—a short, thigh-revealing pouf of fabric—was roundly accepted as the counter to the buttoned-down, conservative, no-time-for-fun 80s alternative. Lacroix echoed the extravagant tastes of the decade by using rich, sumptuous fabrics like velvet and silk and making lavish use of embroidery. Naturally, Hollywood gravitated toward such blatant luxury—Lacroix's famous customers include Sigourney Weaver and Kristin Scott Thomas.

BOB MACKIE (1940–)

Outrageous at the Oscars

It is next to impossible to discuss Oscar fashion without mentioning Bob Mackie. Perhaps best known as the man behind many of Cher's most outrageous Oscar-night outfits, Mackie has also dressed Sally Field, Ann-Margret, Oprah Winfrey and Madonna. The native Californian made his mark on Hollywood first, then launched his own ready-to-wear line, accessible to anyone eager to bring a touch of Hollywood glamour to her closet. He is known for imaginative, unusual evening gowns, and a star knows that if she wears a Mackie creation on the red carpet, she's bound to be an original.

19*80* HAIR APPARENT

52ND
ACADEMY AWARDS
April 14, 1980
Dorothy Chandler Pavilion
Los Angeles
HOST: JOHNNY CARSON

The first year of the decade showed stars saying goodbye to the more natural, experimental looks of the 70s and hello to more conservative, status-oriented ensembles. Hemlines might have been all over the place, but one thing was for sure—hair was getting bigger. Much bigger.

AND THE OSCAR® GOES TO...

Best Picture:
Kramer vs. Kramer

Best Director:
Robert Benton,
Kramer vs. Kramer

Best Actress:
Sally Field,
Norma Rae

Best Actor:
Dustin Hoffman,
Kramer vs. Kramer

Best Supporting Actress:
Meryl Streep,
Kramer vs. Kramer

Best Supporting Actor:
Melvyn Douglas,
Being There

LAST DAYS OF DISCO

Lauren Hutton (with **Telly Savalas**) breezed into the show wearing a gold lamé sweatshirt with matching shorts. The glitzy fabric recalled 70s disco fashions, but the sweatshirt material was a natural choice given the 80s' obsession with aerobics and fitness.

©A.M.P.A.S.®

FIELDS OF GOLD

Perhaps trying not to look too hopeful, **Sally Field** took a conservative approach when choosing this Bob Mackie white suit with a colorful beaded chiffon blouse. The outfit was more suited to a luncheon than to what turned out to be a big night for the star—she took home the Oscar for Best Actress for her role in *Norma Rae*. With her is Best Actor **Dustin Hoffman**.

REPEAT PERFORMANCE?

Wearing a gown that looks suspiciously like the red Valentino Elizabeth Taylor wore in 1976, **Jamie Lee Curtis** is strikingly elegant in this strapless gown with matching scarf.

PERFECT TEN

Bo Derek is California cool in this white tunic that fades into dusky rose on the sleeves. This au naturel look is clearly a holdover from the 70s.

A WIDE WINGSPAN

This pleated, sequined gown features a glittering belt and swaths of fabric that swing out from the shoulder and hip, making **Ann-Margret** look like she's going to fly away.

BAT GIRL

Marisa Berenson (with **Dennis Christopher**) ushers in the 80s with a black, bat-winged bloused gown and mismatched accessories: a wide gold belt and chunky white necklace.

FLASHDANCE

Edy Williams just loves to show off—this time, it's in a two-piece skirt-and-vest combo held together very loosely over sequined bikini briefs.

PRESIDENTIAL PARDON 19**81**

After being postponed a day following the assassination attempt on President Ronald Reagan, the Oscars went forward without a hitch—unless you count the awkward fashions that paraded down the red carpet. The stars were in tune with the looks the rest of the country was sporting, but in putting its own glitzy spin on 80s trends, Hollywood was king when it came to ostentatious outfits.

53RD
ACADEMY AWARDS
March 31, 1981
Dorothy Chandler Pavilion
Los Angeles
HOST: JOHNNY CARSON

©A.M.P.A.S.®

©A.M.P.A.S.®

AND THE OSCAR® GOES TO...

Best Picture:
Ordinary People

Best Director:
Robert Redford,
Ordinary People

Best Actress:
Sissy Spacek,
Coal Miner's Daughter

Best Actor:
Robert De Niro,
Raging Bull

Best Supporting Actress:
Mary Steenburgen,
Melvin and Howard

Best Supporting Actor:
Timothy Hutton,
Ordinary People

NO ORDINARY PEOPLE

Mary Tyler Moore beamed as **Timothy Hutton**, her costar in the film *Ordinary People*, won the Oscar for Best Supporting Actor. She wears an asymmetrical, heavily beaded lavender evening gown with an oversized lavender bow at the waist. Yes, that gigantic white pouf of fabric is what passed for a sleeve in the fashion-challenged 80s.

SPACE SUIT

Sissy Spacek picked up a Best Actress Oscar in a black pantsuit flecked with silver and gold pinstripes. The suit featured full legs that tapered at the ankles, a silhouette that would come to dominate the 80s.

1981

ICY STARE

Sigourney Weaver's pantsuit drapes over her shoulder pads and arms like melting ice cream; **Nastassja Kinski's** raspberry sorbet-colored off-the-shoulder gown shimmers beside her.

STAR STRUCK

Jane Seymour flashes an emotionless, deer-in-the-headlights glare in this one-sleeved, candy-apple-red gown glittering with silver strands. Note the future medicine woman's very big, very 80s hair.

SKIN TIGHT

Bernadette Peters may have big hair, but she's keeping her dress small. This figure-hugging gown is in a shade so close to her complexion it almost blends in with her skin. She poses alongside **Billy Dee Williams**.

BLACK AND WHITE BALL

Margot Kidder and **Lesley-Ann Down** dress like polar opposites: Kidder gets dramatic in a black, high-necked lace gown, while Down takes her neckline lower in an off-the-shoulder, pouf-sleeved, sweet-sixteen-style dress.

WHAT SHE WORE WAS HARD TO IGNORE

Angie Dickinson's gown bears one of the hallmarks of 80s fashion: a gaudy, hard-to-ignore (even if you tried) color.

19**82** PUMP UP THE VOLUME

The 80s were forging an identity, and the stars reflected the national frenzy for bigger, better and brasher everything: hair, gowns, jewelry—even breasts were getting bigger, thanks to the new implants fad. It seemed like the only thing on stage that wasn't getting bigger was the Oscar statue itself.

54TH
ACADEMY AWARDS
March 29, 1982
Dorothy Chandler Pavilion
Los Angeles
HOST: JOHNNY CARSON

AND THE OSCAR® GOES TO...

Best Picture:
Chariots of Fire

Best Director:
Warren Beatty,
Reds

Best Actress:
Katharine Hepburn,
On Golden Pond

Best Actor:
Henry Fonda,
On Golden Pond

Best Supporting Actress:
Maureen Stapleton,
Reds

Best Supporting Actor:
John Gielgud,
Arthur

EYES SKYWARD

Meryl Streep (with husband **Don Gummer**) wears a gown with a ruffled flourish at the sleeve and a tight bodice. In typical 80s style, her normally straight hair has been curled, most likely in an attempt to make it bigger and bolder— or perhaps just to match the poufs in her sleeves.

RAIDER OF THE WRONG CLOSET

In her corseted, gold-ribboned, puff-sleeved top and ruffled black skirt, **Karen Allen** appears to have taken a wrong turn on the way to good taste.

CUDDLING OSCAR

Maureen Stapleton's midnight-blue, sheer-sleeved gown is offset by a dazzling diamond necklace and a mane of silvery-white hair.

©A.M.P.A.S.®

©A.M.P.A.S.®

WINGING IT

Debra Winger looks ready to attend her prom in this ill-fitting lace-and-satin gown. The high collar and strategically placed lace were no doubt intended to be sexy, but the sheer netting and lacy appliqués just look dowdy.

JUST A GOOD OL' BOY

John Schneider does indeed look like a duke in this traditional evening tux—he's even got a pair of white gloves sticking out of his breast pocket!

TUNESMITHS

©A.M.P.A.S.®

Burt Bacharach, **Carole Bayer Sager** and **Christopher Cross** beam after winning the Oscar for Best Song for writing "Arthur's Theme." The men are decked out in tuxes, while Sager wears a suitably sexy floor-length, seashell pink gown with a low neckline.

STAYING ALIVE

©A.M.P.A.S.®

John Travolta helps pay tribute to **Barbara Stanwyck** by presenting her with the Honorary Oscar. The screen legend wears a beaded red evening gown that complements her still-radiant complexion.

SMALL STARS, BIG NIGHT 1983

A little alien had won the hearts of moviegoers everywhere, but it was E.T.'s young onscreen costar who drew the most attention on Oscar night. Little Drew Barrymore brought old-fashioned glamour back to the awards in her fairy-princess gown.

55TH
ACADEMY AWARDS
April 11, 1983
Dorothy Chandler Pavilion
Los Angeles
HOSTS: VARIOUS

AND THE OSCAR® GOES TO...

Best Picture:
Gandhi

Best Director:
Richard Attenborough,
Gandhi

Best Actress:
Meryl Streep,
Sophie's Choice

Best Actor:
Ben Kingsley,
Gandhi

Best Supporting Actress:
Jessica Lange,
Tootsie

Best Supporting Actor:
Louis Gossett Jr.,
An Officer and a Gentleman

BLUE BELLE

In a knee-length aqua-blue Valentino strewn with sequins, Best Supporting Actress-winner **Jessica Lange** evokes the heart and soul of 80s fashion. The shoulder pads, look-at-me color and practical, above-the-knee hemline were adopted from the wardrobes of working women across the country.

LITTLE PRINCESS

Drew Barrymore is as precious as a princess in a hot-pink, two-tiered gown and a white fur stole as she smiles for photographers with mother **Jaid** in tow.

FLEXING THEIR MUSCLES

Meryl Streep's choice in fashion this year was a delicately beaded, loose tunic, not unlike something that the Indian countrywomen of **Ben Kingsley's** Gandhi might wear. Kingsley, who broke with tradition and wore a white tuxedo, won the Best Actor Oscar for his portrayal of Gandhi in the film of the same name.

©A.M.P.A.S.®

TEEN DREAM

Teenaged screen-queen **Kristy McNichol** turns out in an androgynous outfit, a white tux with feminine touches—lavender lapels, bow tie and cummerbund.

DRESSED DOWN

Cher (with **Placido Domingo** to her left) plays the subtlety card (surprisingly) in this floor-length glittering white sheath—it kept her covered all the way up to the boat-neck neckline.

©A.M.P.A.S.®

CLASSICALLY BEAUTIFUL

If **Jamie Lee Curtis's** gown looks like a classic from the 40s, that's because it is: this fitted, below-the-knee dress was once worn by Marlene Dietrich.

BLACK BEAUTY

Raquel Welch tones it down in a subdued, off-the-shoulder black gown that tastefully displays her famous figure.

©A.M.P.A.S.®

19*84* FASHION GETS TURNED UPSIDE DOWN

In the first few minutes of the ceremony's television broadcast this year, the stars' well-chosen outfits suddenly seemed all for naught, as the footage of celebrities strolling down the red carpet was shown upside down. Fortunately, the mistake was soon righted, and the stars were able to trot out their selections on TV for all the world to see—the right way.

56TH
ACADEMY AWARDS
April 9, 1984
Dorothy Chandler Pavilion
Los Angeles
HOST: JOHNNY CARSON

AND THE OSCAR® GOES TO...

Best Picture:
Terms of Endearment

Best Director:
James L. Brooks,
Terms of Endearment

Best Actress:
Shirley MacLaine,
Terms of Endearment

Best Actor:
Robert Duvall,
Tender Mercies

Best Supporting Actress:
Linda Hunt,
The Year of Living Dangerously

Best Supporting Actor:
Jack Nicholson,
Terms of Endearment

CHANNELING THE GOLDEN GIRLS

Best Actress-winner **Shirley MacLaine** sparkles in a beaded evening gown with matching cardigan in the pale pink shade favored by many Florida retirees. The shoulder pads bulking up her frame were staples of 80s fashion.

©A.M.P.A.S.®

MINNELLI IN MAGENTA

Liza Minnelli offsets her inky black hair in a deep magenta sheath with matching evening purse and a black-and-magenta scarf.

LIVING DANGEROUSLY

Best Supporting Actress-winner **Linda Hunt** plays up her smaller stature in an ethnic-inspired tunic and pageboy haircut.

LEAVING FOR LAS VEGAS

Amy Irving's white gown with pagoda shoulders and high neck gives the impression that she and **Steven Spielberg** headed straight from the altar to the ceremony. In reality, they wouldn't be married until the fall of 1985.

ALEXANDER THE GREAT

This royal blue off-the-shoulder gown with regal details like a portrait neckline, oversized peplum and contrasting cuffs gives **Jane Alexander** the royal treatment.

1984

SPLASH OF COLOR

Daryl Hannah is sure to attract attention in this aqua-blue, backless gown emblazoned with a giant bow.

HAVE MERCY

©A.M.P.A.S.®

Remember when skinny ties were big? Even though **Robert Duvall's** tux tie isn't printed with piano keys, it's a pretty unusual choice for Oscar night.

©A.M.P.A.S.®

ROCK ME, AMADEUS 1985

It was too bad the film about Mozart didn't influence fashion this year—more than a few attendees would have benefited from slapping a wig over their outsized hairdos. But the fashion at the time was for high hair, and Hollywood, of course, had to have the highest.

57TH
ACADEMY AWARDS
March 25, 1985
Dorothy Chandler Pavilion
Los Angeles
HOST: JACK LEMMON

©A.M.P.A.S.®

A PLACE IN OUR HEARTS
Sally Field wore a black, strapless gown with a bow-shaped diamond necklace when giving her famous, "You like me!" speech.

ALL THAT GLITTERS
Everyone wondered where **Stevie Wonder** found this terrific tuxedo: the lapels sparkle with red, green, blue and gold sequins, and a matching red shirt peeks out from beneath the jacket.

©A.M.P.A.S.®

BRONZE BEAUTY
Candice Bergen (with **Louis Malle**) arrives at the Oscars in a shiny bronze shift—accessorized, of course, with big earrings and big hair.

AND THE OSCAR® GOES TO...

Best Picture:
Amadeus

Best Director:
Milos Forman,
Amadeus

Best Actress:
Sally Field,
Places in the Heart

Best Actor:
F. Murray Abraham,
Amadeus

Best Supporting Actress:
Peggy Ashcroft,
A Passage to India

Best Supporting Actor:
Haing S. Ngor,
The Killing Fields

©A.M.P.A.S.®

SPOTLIGHT
on Gowns: 1980s

When all is said and done, there is one good thing that came out of the 80s: they ended, and fashion returned to its senses. Ugly outfits went the way of Boy George and *Miami Vice*, and we got our classically beautiful celebrities back. But, mindful of the maxim that says those who forget history are doomed to repeat it, let's deconstruct exactly what went wrong in the "gimme" decade.

1981

SISSY SPACEK SUITED UP

The jumpsuit Sissy Spacek wore to the 1981 Oscars was as black as the night sky and shot through with metallic threads—a bold, new look where no woman had gone before.

Since this outfit is from the early 80s, Sissy Spacek has retained a more 70s-influenced *natural and straight hairstyle.*

Shoulder pads and a loose, blouson top were common features in 80s fashion.

The pants begin *high on the waist, balloon out at the thigh, then taper at the ankle.* This was considered a desirable silhouette at the time.

Bigger, bolder, brasher: even a dark pantsuit had to have a little bit of flash— here in the form of *silver and gold pinstripes*—in order to be considered fashionable.

Interestingly, styles for evening shoes haven't changed all that much over the years. These *open-toed, high-heeled sandals* are not unlike the evening shoes women wear today.

©A.M.P.A.S.®

JESSICA LANGE BLUE CRUSH

VALENTINO

1983

Jessica Lange's ice-blue Valentino was a veritable crash course in 1980s styling. The shape, cut and color of the dress could only have worked in the 80s.

Lange's *big, curled hair* made her a fashionable lady in the heyday of the 80s.

Ah, the ubiquitous *shoulder pads*. No outfit was complete without them. Like Spacek's, Lange's top is slightly oversized—shoulder pads give it shape and make it hang on the body in that oh-so-80s way.

Sparkle and flash were the most desirable aspects of any fabric from the 1980s. The "diamonds" scattered about this short gown give it the requisite glitter.

This skirt falls to *just above the knee*, an echo of the "power suits" being worn by women across the country as they entered the workforce. A shorter hemline—but not too short—showed that a woman meant business.

Matching *shiny aqua-blue* shoes finished off the look.

©A.M.P.A.S.®

OLIVIA NEWTON-JOHN
HOPELESSLY OUT OF FASHION

Australian pop singer Olivia Newton-John and her husband, Matt Lattanzi, for better or for worse, really nailed 80s fashion.

Big, blonde hair made any girl a pinup in the "bigger is better" 80s.

An *extra-wide collar* in white lace contrasted with the shiny black material of the rest of the gown. Exaggerated details such as this collar were a common feature of 80s styles.

By the end of the decade, *tight-fitting garments* had come back into fashion, as evidenced by this fitted bodice. Blouses were no longer "in" when it came to evening wear.

Big, silver buttons fit in with the "more is more" mentality of the decade.

To match her extra-wide collar, Newton-John had to have an equally *voluminous skirt*, an ironic throwback to the 50s style of dressing.

1989

*19**86*** OUT OF FASHION

Nobody can beat Cher for the sheer … well, for the sheerness of her Oscar–night outfits, for one, but also for her utter willingness to push the fashion envelope each and every time she arrives at the Academy Awards. This year, she took her Academy Awards aesthetic to new heights.

58TH
ACADEMY AWARDS
March 24, 1986
Dorothy Chandler Pavilion
Los Angeles
HOSTS: ALAN ALDA
JANE FONDA
ROBIN WILLIAMS

AND THE OSCAR® GOES TO…

Best Picture:
Out of Africa

Best Director:
Sydney Pollack,
Out of Africa

Best Actress
Geraldine Page,
The Trip to Bountiful

Best Actor:
William Hurt,
Kiss of the Spider Woman

Best Supporting Actress:
Anjelica Huston,
Prizzi's Honor

Best Supporting Actor:
Don Ameche,
Cocoon

MACKIE ME OVER

Cher shows plenty of skin in this Bob Mackie-designed ensemble that was undoubtedly the most talked about outfit on the red carpet in 1986. The attention-getting headdress is made of rooster feathers and measures two feet from top to bottom. With her is Best Supporting Actor **Don Ameche**.

©A.M.P.A.S.®

SHE'LL LIVE FOREVER

Irene Cara found fame in this prime example of 80s styling: big, broad shoulders created by the ever-present shoulder pads, long, dangling earrings, and oversized baubles form this tribute to excess.
©A.M.P.A.S.®

LADY IN RED

Lionel Richie and his wife, **Brenda,** might have felt like dancing on the ceiling after Richie won the Oscar for his song "Say You, Say Me." He sports a tuxedo jacket featuring a shawl collar, and she wears a lacy red gown with matching long scarf.

©A.M.P.A.S.®

SHEEDY'S GOT IT

Ally Sheedy packed herself into this two-piece gown for her 1986 appearance. She looks anything but bratty in the shimmering white halter-style top with matching skirt.

GORGEOUS IN GREEN

Anjelica Huston collaborated with designer Tzetzi Ganev to create this one-of-a-kind emerald-green crepe gown. She accessorized with a white fur stole and date **Jack Nicholson.**

©A.M.P.A.S.®

SIXTEEN CANDLES

Molly Ringwald is pretty in black as she attends the show with **Dweezil Zappa**. The teen sensation's elegant gown features a sheer black overlay and lace-edged sleeves.

RISKY BUSINESS

Starlet **Rebecca De Mornay** took a chance by wearing this frumpy draped gown with a matching coat that was easy to ignore. Her well-sprayed hair, on the other hand, was hard to miss.

TIGHTENING THEIR BELTS 1987

Platoon **won the Oscar for Best Picture**, but as usual, all eyes were on the red carpet as the 80s reached their apogee. The frills and baubles of the first half of the decade were giving way to more aggressively tight, figure-revealing clothes.

59TH
ACADEMY AWARDS
March 31, 1987
Dorothy Chandler Pavilion
Los Angeles

HOSTS: CHEVY CHASE
GOLDIE HAWN
PAUL HOGAN

AND
THE OSCAR®
GOES TO...

Best Picture:
Platoon

Best Director:
Oliver Stone,
Platoon

Best Actress:
Marlee Matlin,
Children of a Lesser God

Best Actor:
Paul Newman,
The Color of Money

Best Supporting Actress:
Dianne Wiest,
Hannah and Her Sisters

Best Supporting Actor:
Michael Caine,
Hannah and Her Sisters

©A.M.P.A.S.®

PINK LADY
This pink taffeta number with its tight, boned bodice and puffed sleeves gave even the glamorous **Elizabeth Taylor** the 80s treatment. Note her high, teased hair, touched with streaks of gray. With her are Oscar-winners **Arnold Kopelman** (left) and **Oliver Stone**.

MATTHEW BRODERICK'S DAY OFF
Rising star **Matthew Broderick** arrives at the awards with fellow actor **Jennifer Grey**, whose off-the-shoulder, deep-blue jersey dress shows off her California tan and golden hair.

123

1987

GIFT OF THE MARY
Mary Elizabeth Mastrantonio looks ready to be unwrapped in this big-shouldered ivory gown with a giant bow at the low-slung waist.

POUF PASTRY
Rita Wilson (with husband **Tom Hanks**) flounces down the red carpet in this strapless white gown with a pouf of fabric for a skirt.

BLUE VELVET

A velvety smooth gown gives **Isabella Rossellini** the look of low-key glamour. A wide neckline revealing a sliver of pale skin contrasts with the deep blue of the gown.

SILVER STREAK

Oprah Winfrey looks more like an extra for the Ice Capades than a serious celebrity in this misguided Bob Mackie creation.

BRAGGING RIGHTS

Sonia Braga hits the right note with this strapless, beaded gown. The swirls and peaked bustline might look dated today, but in 1987 this gown was a winner.

1988

STARSTUCK

60TH
ACADEMY AWARDS
April 11, 1988
Shrine Auditorium
Los Angeles
HOST: CHEVY CHASE

Fashion was dealt a blow this year when many of the attendees had to walk to the ceremony after their limos got stuck in a massive traffic jam on a hot L. A. evening. Sweltering heat is never comfortable, but it was particularly unwelcome to the stars hiking to the show in their heels and finest silks.

AND THE OSCAR® GOES TO...

Best Picture:
The Last Emperor

Best Director:
Bernardo Bertolucci,
The Last Emperor

Best Actress:
Cher,
Moonstruck

Best Actor:
Michael Douglas,
Wall Street

Best Supporting Actress:
Olympia Dukakis,
Moonstruck

Best Supporting Actor:
Sean Connery,
The Untouchables

THUMBS UP

Marlee Matlin stands with Best Oscar-winner **Michael Douglas**. She wears a strapless, off-the-rack gown in a vivid shade of pink garnished with a huge bow at the waist, a hallmark of 80s style.

©A.M.P.A.S.®

DRAMATIC DUO

Documentary filmmakers **Sue Marx** and **Pamela Conn** laugh as they leave the podium with their Oscars. Marx wears a lavender tunic with a matching fringed scarf; Conn embodies the power-dressing look in her shoulder-padded, pleated blue jersey gown.

©A.M.P.A.S.®

126

LITTLE TO HIDE

Cher gives the people what they want once again in this see-through gown made of silk netting. She didn't remove her robe until she reached the podium, ensuring that all eyes were on her as she showed off yet another of her headline-making Bob Mackie gowns.

©A.M.P.A.S.®

OSCAR ALOFT

Best Supporting Actress-winner **Olympia Dukakis** holds her Oscar high after winning for her role in *Moonstruck*. Her black lace gown with elaborate flounces at the shoulders incorporates all the flashiness of typical 80s creations.

©A.M.P.A.S.®

1988

SPOT ON

Only **Audrey Hepburn** could pull off pairing polka dots with stripes. This black-and-white gown manages to incorporate elements of 80s style, like the two-tiered skirt, without succumbing to poor taste.

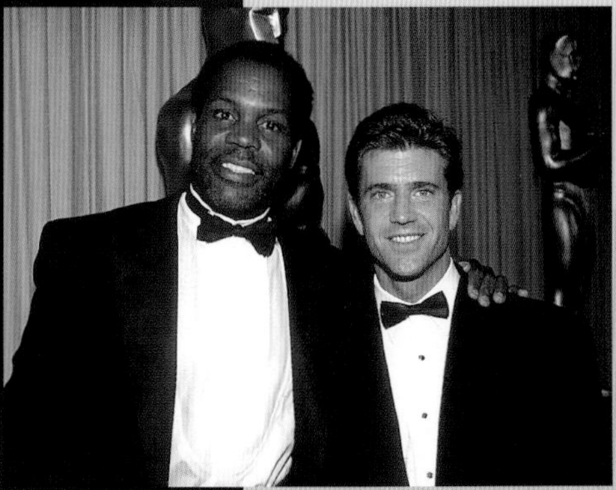

LETHAL WEAPONS

©A.M.P.A.S.®

Kings of the 1980s buddy movie, **Danny Glover** and **Mel Gibson** matched up nicely in their traditional tuxedos.

BACK IN BLACK

Holly Hunter's short, black, strapless dress matches her date's tuxedo but does little to flatter her figure.

©A.M.P.A.S.®

OUT WITH A BANG 19*89*

The decade was drawing to a close, and the 90s were soon to usher in a return to minimalism. But 80s style would linger for a few more years, and in this, the last year of the Oscars in the 80s, the stars displayed the most diversity yet. Pantsuits, long gowns, short skirts paired with shirts—it was a fashion free-for-all on the red carpet.

61ST
ACADEMY AWARDS
April 29, 1989
Shrine Auditorium
Los Angeles
HOST: ROBIN WILLIAMS

©A.M.P.A.S.®

AND THE OSCAR® GOES TO...

Best Picture:
Rain Man

Best Director:
Barry Levinson,
Rain Man

Best Actress:
Jodie Foster,
The Accused

Best Actor:
Dustin Hoffman,
Rain Man

Best Supporting Actress:
Geena Davis,
The Accidental Tourist

Best Supporting Actor:
Kevin Kline,
A Fish Called Wanda

SQUARE PEGS

Long before *Sex and the City* made her star rise and frequent trips to rehab made his fall, **Sarah Jessica Parker** and **Robert Downey Jr.** attended the Academy Awards together in true 80s style. She's got big, curly hair piled on top of her head and a short dress, and he looks a little different than all the other gents in a green tie and belt.

SHE'S SO VAIN

Actually, vanity may not have been on **Carly Simon's** mind when she decided to don this striped blue and gold suit with an extra-wide lapel. Luckily, her songwriting skills fared better than her sartorial sense, earning her an Oscar for "Let the River Run" from the film *Working Girl*.

1989

TEXAS-SIZED HAIR

Natural beauties **Candice Bergen** and **Jacqueline Bisset** shimmer in glittering gowns. Bisset wears a pale-green, off-the-shoulder gown with a ruched waist panel, while Bergen sparkles in a pink gown topped by a beaded, masculine, button-down shirt. Both women also chose big earrings and enough hairspray to keep their 'dos pointing skyward all evening.

WORK IT, GIRL

Melanie Griffith, nominated for Best Actress for her role in *Working Girl*, arrives at the ceremony with long-term love **Don Johnson**. Griffith's low-cut gown is embellished with huge off-the-shoulder ruffles and a choker with a ruby center. The couple sports matching hairstyles—all big blond feathers.

1989

COOL DUDES

Michelle Pfeiffer is quietly cool in a navy-blue crepe suit by Armani as she stands beside **Dennis Quaid**, who sports sun-bleached locks.

DRESS REHEARSAL

Winona Ryder and **Christian Slater** get gussied up, 80s-style: she wears a spaghetti-strapped short dress with black stockings—a far cry from the glamorous getups she'll stroll the red carpet in throughout the 90s and beyond.

©A.M.P.A.S.®

DUCK AND COVER

Angie Dickinson may have been foreshadowing Bjork's infamous 2002 "duck" dress when she donned this stinker. But nevermind the dress—take a look at those uber-80s earrings!

Oscar's Most Beautiful Gowns

Throughout the annals of Oscar history, many beautiful people have sauntered up the red carpet with style and grace. But a handful of actresses have pulled off looks so captivating that they'll forever be remembered. And it isn't just the gowns that make these women look so ravishing, it's the whole ensemble—a hairstyle or subtle choice of jewelry can often make or break an outfit. Here we present a pageant of positively beguiling looks from 75 years on the red carpet.

1930

ORIGINAL ELEGANCE

Mary Pickford's luminous 1930 gown is truly an original. The craftsmanship required to create such exquisite detailing is rarely seen at the modern Oscars. (See page 22 for more about this gown.)

1954

IT'S A CINCH

Audrey Hepburn's Givenchy-designed gown was a trendsetter in its day, and perfectly suited the gamine star who wore it.

1955

REGAL BEAUTY

Grace Kelly's blue-champagne silk gown, designed by famous studio designer Edith Head, was accessorized with white evening gloves and an embroidered purse to create this magical, winning look. With her is **Marlon Brando**.

1976

RED ZONE

Liz Taylor embodied sophisticated glamour in this strapless Halston gown. The shade of red so suited the actress that the designer forever after referred to it as "Elizabeth Taylor red." The gown upped the ante when it came to picking a knockout Oscar outfit, although this kind of understated elegance didn't become commonplace until the mid-90s. (See page 90 for a color shot.)

1999

BUCOLIC FROLIC

John Galliano designed this enchanting purple knit gown for Oscar-contender **Cate Blanchett**. The sheer back panel, embroidered with hummingbirds and flowers, lent a pastoral feel to the glamorous gown.

2001

GOLDEN GIRL

A zesty lemon-yellow vintage gown from the 1950s gave girl-next-door **Renée Zellweger** a shot of old-fashioned glamour. Her wavy blonde hair and red lips complete the screen-siren look.

2002

HOLY BERRY

Halle Berry turned heads and had fashion critics raving for days after she wore this enthralling deep-red silk taffeta gown designed by Elie Saab. The strategically embroidered mesh top and the full, richly-hued skirt were dramatic counterpoints to Berry's fresh, good looks.

THE *1990s*

AS GOOD AS IT GETS

As if embarrassed by the riches of the previous decade, fashion took a sharp turn in the 90s and veered towards a brand-new look—minimalism. As the stock market flagged, conspicuous displays of wealth became something to frown upon: less really was more. Restrained basics formed the core of every actor's wardrobe, and it was common to see actresses walking around L.A. in sneakers instead of stilettos. Indeed, many actresses had given over the job of looking like a glamour puss 'round the clock to supermodels. Nevertheless, nothing stopped the stars from dressing to the hilt on Oscar night. In fact, even though big hair and ostentatious designs had gone out of fashion, evening wear was enjoying a renaissance, returning to the sophisticated, understated elegance of the 1930s. Actresses understood that true luxury could be found in details such as the quality of material, the finish of a seam and the classic lines of a well-cut dress. It was just such a return to gracefulness that made the 1990s the decade that the Oscars' pre-show fashion parade became as enduringly intriguing as the awards themselves.

FASHION ON FILM

Swingers (1996)

This tale of five friends looking for love in Los Angeles brought the retro Swing–dance craze that had been quietly sweeping the nation to film. Swingers was the antithesis of the grunge movement that marked the early 90s, and showed its young stars dressed in dapper suits, not flannels, and swigging cocktails, not beer.

Pulp Fiction (1994)

Quentin Tarantino's ultra-hip caper restored John Travolta to the limelight and secured independent film's place on the Hollywood map. The film glorified the seedier side of life, and its edgy irreverence influenced mainstream fashion, making stovepipe pants, Goth haircuts and sideburns cool.

DESIGNERS TO THE STARS: 1990s

CALVIN KLEIN (1942–)

Master of Minimalism

New York-born Calvin Klein references the sleek lines and aggressive stance of his hometown in the clothing he designs. He uses muted colors like gray, taupe and aubergine when designing his deceptively simple yet elegant clothes, which always look up to the minute and fresh. His gift for designing clothes is matched only by his genius for marketing his creations in sexy, youthful advertisements that never fail to generate publicity. Stars look to Klein when choosing their Oscar outfits for a serious yet sexy look that won't fail to put them in the spotlight. Some of his famous customers include fashion-forward stars like Gwyneth Paltrow, Susan Sarandon and Sarah Jessica Parker.

GIANNI VERSACE (1946-1997)

King of Glamour

Gianni Versace was born in southern Italy and learned his trade at his mother's feet. He made his mark on the fashion world in the 1980s when he recruited the world's top models to show off his sexy, clinging clothes. He was a master at designing garments splashed with neobaroque patterns and vivid colors in regal shades of gold, royal blue and purple. His trademark, a golden Medusa head, was frequently stamped on his fabrics and line of accessories. Tragically, Versace was murdered in 1997 at the height of his career. His sister Donatella took over the direction of the house of Versace after her brother's death, and celebrities continue to wear Versace gowns whenever they need a jaw-droppingly sexy look. Some of Hollywood's hottest stars, like Ellen Barkin, Elizabeth Hurley and Jennifer Lopez, have worn Versace to the Oscars.

PRADA (1950–)

Fashion's New Wave

Italian Miuccia Prada joined her uncle's leather-goods design company in the late 70s, but it wasn't until the 90s that she found real success as a clothing designer. Prada's funky, youthful styles manage to retain an air of refined elegance and cutting-edge simplicity that is coveted by women around the globe. When Uma Thurman wore Prada's lavender evening gown to the 1995 Oscars, Prada was thrust onto the world fashion map and given a permanent home there. Nicole Kidman and Sigourney Weaver have also attended the Oscars Prada-clad.

ARMANI'S ARMY

Although he had entered the Oscar-dressing scene in the 80s, at the 1990 ceremony it seemed like almost half the attendees were dressed in Giorgio Armani. The 90s' aesthetic—muted, mellow, sophisticated—was off to an elegant start.

62ND
ACADEMY AWARDS
March 26, 1990
Dorothy Chandler Pavilion
Los Angeles
HOST: BILLY CRYSTAL

AND THE OSCAR® GOES TO...

Best Picture:
Driving Miss Daisy

Best Director:
Oliver Stone,
Born on the Fourth of July

Best Actress:
Jessica Tandy,
Driving Miss Daisy

Best Actor:
Daniel Day-Lewis,
My Left Foot

Best Supporting Actress:
Brenda Fricker,
My Left Foot

Best Supporting Actor:
Denzel Washington,
Glory

PRETTY WOMAN
Julia Roberts (with **Kiefer Sutherland**) bares all in this figure-revealing taupe Armani gown with a gathered hem.

NEVER BASIC

Diana Ross wears a sheer black gown, but —unable to settle for
something as boring as black—the supremely fashionable lady
adds a shocking pink wrap.

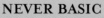
©A.M.P.A.S.®

RED HEAD

Geena Davis (with **Denzel Washington**) was a stunner in this
shirred red silk gown designed by Hollywood costume designer Bill
Hargate. A cluster of pearls around her neck and pearls dangling
from her ears were the perfect complement to this glamorous look.

1990

RED HOT

The dress is clearly moving into 90s territory, but her hair is still stuck in the 80s. Nevertheless, a slinky red columnar gown gives **Elizabeth McGovern** the starlet treatment.

©A.M.P.A.S.®

DANCES IN STYLE *1991*

Dances with Wolves **may have won Kevin Costner Best Picture and Best Director Oscars**, but the Western certainly didn't influence fashion. The stars continued to turn out in glamorous, sleek gowns, as befitted the tasteful new decade.

SCARLET FEVER

Susan Sarandon salutes her fans in a regal scarlet silk crepe gown by Carolyne Roehm. The intense shade of red complements her auburn hair as she strolls alongside companion **Tim Robbins**.

RUNAWAY BRIDE

Julia Roberts looked ready to board a stagecoach in this overwrought Richard Tyler gown. A few days after the award's ceremony, she actually did head for the hills, leaving fiancée **Kiefer Sutherland** high and dry at the altar.

63RD
ACADEMY AWARDS
March 25, 1991
Shrine Auditorium
Los Angeles
HOST: BILLY CRYSTAL

AND THE OSCAR® GOES TO…

Best Picture:
Dances with Wolves

Best Director:
Kevin Costner,
Dances with Wolves

Best Actress:
Kathy Bates,
Misery

Best Actor:
Jeremy Irons,
Reversal of Fortune

Best Supporting Actress:
Whoopi Goldberg,
Ghost

Best Supporting Actor:
Joe Pesci,
GoodFellas

WHOOPING
IT UP

An emotional **Whoopi Goldberg** was the first black actress to earn an Oscar since **Hattie McDaniel** won for *Gone with the Wind* in 1939. Goldberg accepted the monumental award (for Best Supporting Actress in *Ghost)* in a black, sequined, boat neck gown.

©A.M.P.A.S.®

ELEGANCE REVISITED

Annette Bening arrived on the red carpet in a gorgeous gown that was a costume from the set of *Bugsy*, the film the actress was working on the day she appeared as an Oscar presenter. The 40s-style beige beauty is heavily beaded and smartly accessorized with gold shoes and a gold clutch. **Ed Begley, Jr.** stands beside her.

LOREN'S LUSTER

In a floor-sweeping, beaded black Valentino gown with a matching sheer shawl, **Sophia Loren** shows she is well deserving of an honorary Oscar for adding "permanent luster to our art form," as the Academy put it.

©A.M.P.A.S.®

GERE'D UP

Cindy Crawford lives up to the term "supermodel" in this chili-pepper hot Versace gown. She and handsome hubby-to-be **Richard Gere** could have been the hottest couple at the awards show.

1992 YESTERDAY'S LOOKS TODAY

64TH
ACADEMY AWARDS
March 30, 1992
Dorothy Chandler Pavilion
Los Angeles
HOST: BILLY CRYSTAL

As *Silence of the Lambs* **racked up Oscar after Oscar**, there were a few black sheep in the fashion parade. But other stars began a bold new trend: wearing vintage clothing to the Oscars. Winona Ryder is perhaps best known for wearing beautiful old gowns to the awards show, but Amy Irving and Jamie Lee Curtis had already beat her to the punch in the 80s. The trend has since gained popularity with other stars, such as Julia Roberts and Renée Zellweger.

AND THE OSCAR® GOES TO...

Best Picture:
The Silence of the Lambs

Best Director:
Jonathan Demme,
The Silence of the Lambs

Best Actress:
Jodie Foster,
The Silence of the Lambs

Best Actor:
Anthony Hopkins,
The Silence of the Lambs

Best Supporting Actress:
Mercedes Ruehl,
The Fisher King

Best Supporting Actor:
Jack Palance,
City Slickers

CRIMPING HER STYLE

Barbra Streisand's mauve Patricia Lester gown with a matching batwing-sleeved jacket is crimply too much. She even matches the accordion-pleated fabric to her crimped hair—not a winning combination.

RED AHEAD

In a one-shouldered, draped red gown by Givenchy, **Audrey Hepburn** proves once again that good taste is timeless. Her dramatic, long earrings emphasize her swan-like neck.

TWO LEGENDS

Elizabeth Taylor's pristine white gown is set off by the red ribbon she wears to symbolize awareness of the AIDS epidemic. Another screen legend, **Paul Newman**, stands beside her, dashing in a traditional tuxedo.

1992

LILY AND DEMI

A gray-blue vintage gown from the 1940s wraps **Demi Moore** in old-world glamour. She is reported to have found the gown at Lily Et Cie, a well-stocked vintage clothing store in Los Angeles.

A LITTLE CORNY

Cornrows funkify **Juliette Lewis'** vintage gown, but a long strand of pearls keeps it classic.

UNFORGIVING YEAR FOR FASHION FAUX PAS 1993

The stars took some serious fashion missteps this year—it was as if they thought it was 1983, not 1993. Luckily, not everyone took a wrong turn. The new mode of dressing was taking hold, and other stars arrived in sleek gowns that were made for the modern age.

65TH
ACADEMY AWARDS
March 29, 1993
Dorothy Chandler Pavilion
Los Angeles
HOST: BILLY CRYSTAL

©A.M.P.A.S.®

FASHION'S END?
An emerald-green sequined top with matching skirt leaves Best Actress-winner **Emma Thompson** looking like she got lost in the 80s.

BLACK VELVET
Style-setter **Geena Davis** garnered sustained applause when she walked onstage in this stunning black velvet floor-length gown. The unusual, asymmetrically curved neckline influenced Oscar fashion for years to come.

AND THE OSCAR® GOES TO...

Best Picture:
Unforgiven

Best Director:
Clint Eastwood,
Unforgiven

Best Actress:
Emma Thompson,
Howards End

Best Actor:
Al Pacino,
Scent of a Woman

Best Supporting Actress:
Marisa Tomei,
My Cousin Vinny

Best Supporting Actor:
Gene Hackman,
Unforgiven

145

1993

FRENCH KISS

French screen legend **Catherine Deneuve** gets gussied up in a black gown with a fluffy pink neckline.

GROWTH SPURT

Jodie Foster looks prim and proper in a strapless Armani columnar gown embellished with an oversized purple flower-shaped belt.

VINNY'S COUSIN MARISA

There may have been some controversy over **Marisa Tomei's** Best Supporting Actress win, but no one could dispute that she looked *trés chic* in this white silk organza Chanel gown with black piping and lace insets.

A DIFFERENT STRIPE

Denzel Washington's double-breasted evening jacket was designed by Armani; wife **Pauletta** doesn't fare quite as well in her black-and-white striped evening gown.

KLEIN SHINE

Tim Robbins looks away while partner **Susan Sarandon** looks a little bit like Oscar in a shiny gold gown by Calvin Klein.

GARDEN VARIETY

Elizabeth Taylor's less-than-glamorous Valentino gown is a little too mellow-yellow for the glamour queen—only her ornately jeweled necklace reminds us she's a diva.

©A.M.P.A.S.®

1994 FASHION GETS SERIOUS

It was a year honoring serious films, and in turn, the stars got serious when choosing their Oscar night ensembles. Most people played it safe with understated glitter and unfussy colors like silver, black and brown.

66TH
ACADEMY AWARDS
March 21, 1994
Dorothy Chandler Pavilion
Los Angeles
HOST:
WHOOPI GOLDBERG

AND THE OSCAR® GOES TO...

Best Picture:
Schindler's List

Best Director:
Steven Spielberg,
Schindler's List

Best Actress:
Holly Hunter,
The Piano

Best Actor:
Tom Hanks,
Philadelphia

Best Supporting Actress:
Anna Paquin,
The Piano

Best Supporting Actor:
Tommy Lee Jones,
The Fugitive

VELVET EMCEE
Comedienne **Whoopi Goldberg** gets seriously elegant in this rich brown velvet gown with an empire waist and long, fitted sleeves. She was the first woman to host the Oscars on her own.

©A.M.P.A.S.®

SETTLING THE SCORE
Goldie Hawn opted for a simple satin gown from Calvin Klein with nothing but a giant pearl drop necklace for jewelry for her 1994 Oscar appearance. She presented the Oscar to **John Williams** for Best Original Score for *Schindler's List*.

MIXED METAPHORS

Winona Ryder wears a vintage gown from the 1950s with a distinctly 1920s feel. Beaded fringe was a common feature of many dresses from the flapper era, and here it adds a touch of whimsy to a fitted, sexy dress.

STONE ALONE

With her gleaming blonde Marcel curls, **Sharon Stone** could have passed for a flapper, but her black halter-style sequined gown places her squarely in the latter half of the century.

CLOSE TO THE BONE

This floor-length, silver, almost matronly Armani keeps **Glenn Close** well-covered—perhaps to foil any *Fatal Attraction*-like jealousies.

1994

WHAT A WAY TO MAKE A LIVING

You just can't clone the inimitable style and voice of **Dolly Parton**. Shown on stage singing with **James Ingram**, she wears a sexy black number featuring a throwback to 80s style—the giant, unnecessary bow.

IN TUNE

Bruce Springsteen picked up an Oscar for crooning the theme song to the Tom Hanks film *Philadelphia*; songstress **Whitney Houston** presented in an ivory jacket over a peekaboo bit of black lace.

©A.M.P.A.S.®

BARKIN' UP THE RIGHT TREE

Ellen Barkin's sultry good looks are enhanced by this short black shift with a trailing train and sexy, T-strap high heels.

150

FASHION HISTORY IS MADE 1995

This was the year that changed the face of Oscar fashion. When Uma Thurman glided down the red carpet in a beaded lavender gown by Prada, heads turned and eyes widened. Stars of all ages suddenly wanted to give up their clingy, sexy Oscar night outfits and return to a look that was elegant, graceful and understated. With that one gown, Uma and Prada had almost single-handedly turned the red carpet into the world's most watched fashion runway.

67TH
ACADEMY AWARDS
March 27, 1995
Shrine Auditorium
Los Angeles
HOST:
DAVID LETTERMAN

DON'T LEAVE HOME WITHOUT IT

Clever costume designer **Lizzie Gardiner** created this golden gown out of American Express cards. After the show, she didn't just bring home the gold card—she also left with the gold Oscar for Best Costume Design for *The Adventures of Priscilla, Queen of the Desert*.

AND THE OSCAR® GOES TO...

Best Picture:
Forrest Gump

Best Director:
Robert Zemeckis,
Forrest Gump

Best Actress:
Jessica Lange,
Blue Sky

Best Actor:
Tom Hanks,
Forrest Gump

Best Supporting Actress:
Dianne Wiest,
Bullets Over Broadway

Best Supporting Actor:
Martin Landau,
Ed Wood

THE GOWN THAT LAUNCHED A THOUSAND IMITATIONS

Uma Thurman's beaded lavender Prada gown features princess seams so that it flows naturally around the actress's figure. Thurman wears a beaded chiffon stole over the delicately pretty gown and a sparkling diamond necklace.

SHEER ENERGY

Holly Hunter waves to the crowds in a sheer Vera Wang with bridal buttons running up the side. She kept the look G-rated thanks to the sequined bra sewn inside.

1995

EXCHANGING PEASANTRIES

A crimson gown embellished with black embroidery and a matching cape gives **Andie McDowell** (with husband **Paul**) a dressed-up peasant vibe.

THE COLOR OF STONE

Sharon Stone's full-skirted Vera Wang gown with a beaded bodice looks like a pewter-colored wedding dress—which is little surprise, as brides are designer Wang's primary clientele.

RATINGS SWEEP

Oprah Winfrey makes a sweeping entrance in a glamorous brown gown. The rich color of the silk organza Gianfranco Ferré contrasts beautifully with her glittering diamond earrings and necklace.

VERY BASIC BLACK

Sarah Jessica Parker (with **Matt Dillon**) is sexy in the city in a sophisticated straight black strapless gown with matching wrap and golden ringlets.

TOO SWEET

A violet Valentino in velvet and silk flattered her figure, but its saccharine aftertaste made **Halle Berry's** selection a bit hard to take.

ARMANI IN LOS ANGELES

Jodie Foster arrives in a high-collared, intricately beaded sheath by Armani. The respected actress has fostered a long relationship with Armani, and frequently attends the Oscars swathed in his creations.

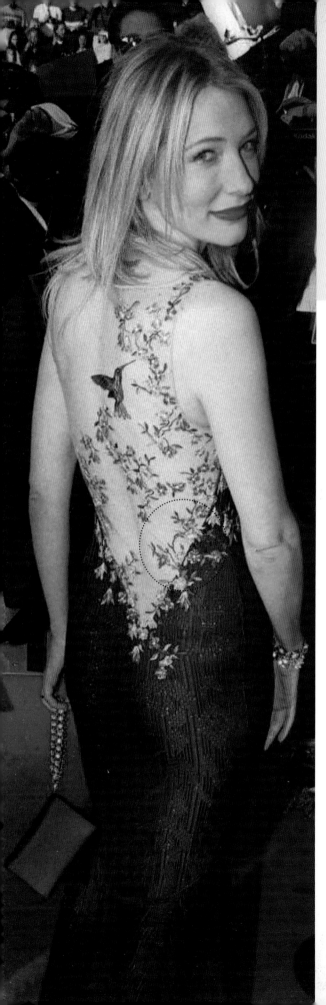

SPOTLIGHT
on Gowns: 1999s

As minimalism came back into fashion in the 90s, so too did good taste. Actresses were courted by the top couture designers to wear their creations in a win-win deal for both: the designers got free publicity and increased name recognition, and actresses, with more fashion muscle behind them, made fewer mistakes on the red carpet. It all translated into a feast for the eyes for fashion aficionados.

CATE BLANCHETT
CATE TAKES A WALK IN THE COUNTRYSIDE

Cate Blanchett's John Galliano gown was one of the most unusual creations to make its way down the red carpet in nearly 70 years. The English actress, with her svelte figure and chameleon-like qualities, pulled the look off with aplomb.

To match the pastoral, English-countryside feel of the gown, Blanchett let her *blonde hair fall naturally* around her face.

The back of the gown was *hand-embroidered in France* with delicate flowers and a busy hummingbird.

The *purple knit fabric* clings to Cate's curves and emphasizes her figure.

The gown features a *slight train*, festooned with a wayward hummingbird. Trains of varying length became a popular feature on gowns during the latter half of the 90s and beyond.

1999

HALLE BERRY
HALLE SAYS 'I DO' TO A BODY-HUGGING VERA WANG

Halle Berry is shaping up to be one of the best-dressed actresses to walk the red carpet. She consistently arrives in form-fitting gowns that show off her extraordinary figure, and she's unafraid to try new designers.

Berry opted for a playful look with *upswept hair* pinned around the crown.

Berry tends to wear little jewelry at her Oscar appearances; here, she wears only *diamond-studded hoop earrings*, and leaves her neck bare.

The pistachio satin Vera Wang is *cut on the bias* and falls gracefully around Berry's waist and hips before cascading to the floor.

Diagonal *insets of see-through lace trim* add interest to an otherwise simply cut gown.

1996

Lace trim *strategically cuts across the lower back*, framing the rear view.

NICOLE KIDMAN
KIDMAN WINS THE PURPLE HEART FOR BRAVERY IN FASHION

The year after Uma Thurman wore her groundbreaking Prada gown, **Nicole Kidman** followed suit in a pale-purple floor-length gown. The Italian designer was gaining a reputation for designing softly romantic yet elegant evening gowns, perfect for actresses who wanted to stand out among the hyper-glamorous Oscar-night crowd.

Kidman twisted her hair into a *low chignon in the back*, and let loose strands frame her face, an echo of the high-low essence of the gown.

Dangling earrings and a *dazzling choker necklace* frame her face but don't distract from the unusual neckline of the gown.

Most of the detail is focused at the bustline; the *empire waist* is underlined with contrasting seaming, as is the neckline.

The gown falls all the way to the floor, accentuating Kidman's long-legged, *statuesque figure*.

PRADA

Just before it covers Kidman's shoes, the gown is edged with *yet another seam*, gathering the floating skirt in and giving it a leaner silhouette.

1996

1996 BRAVE ART

Mel Gibson's epic *Braveheart* **nearly swept the awards,** but the real action was on the red carpet. So large a role was fashion taking at the awards, E! Entertainment Television stationed Joan Rivers on the red carpet for the first time specifically to report on what the stars were wearing. As if oblivious to all the hoopla, the stars rolled into the show on a wave of restrained elegance.

68TH
ACADEMY AWARDS
March 25, 1996
Dorothy Chandler Pavilion
Los Angeles
HOST:
WHOOPI GOLDBERG

AND THE OSCAR® GOES TO...

Best Picture:
Braveheart

Best Director:
Mel Gibson,
Braveheart

Best Actress:
Susan Sarandon,
Dead Man Walking

Best Actor:
Nicolas Cage,
Leaving Las Vegas

Best Supporting Actress:
Mira Sorvino,
Mighty Aphrodite

Best Supporting Actor:
Kevin Spacey,
The Usual Suspects

COOL COUPLE
Brad Pitt and **Gwyneth Paltrow** arrive casually cool, she in a sleek, beaded Calvin Klein, he with an open neckline—no ties bind this guy.

WEST WITH THE NIGHT
Kate Winslet's winsome pink Vivienne Westwood gown flatters her figure and complements her complexion. The chandelier diamond necklace and red wrap are edgy accessories.

DIAMOND GIRL

Angela Bassett sparkled in more than $7 million worth of diamonds, including a 270-carat Harry Winston necklace. Not that anyone noticed, but her low-cut black spaghetti-strapped gown was pretty nice, too.

A SHUE-IN

An ivory satin dress with a train designed by Felicia Farr puts a spring in **Elisabeth Shue's** step as she arrives at the show. The twisted shoulder straps help give the corseted bodice a lift.

BELL BOTTOM

Susan Sarandon's outsized gown recalls the belle epoque look made famous by Christian Dior in the 1950s, but the bronzey-coppery Dolce & Gabbana creation was thoroughly modern—a unique folding technique gave the skirt volume, instead of cumbersome petticoats or wire.

©A.M.P.A.S.®

MIGHTY MIRA

A silver beaded bodice and striped skirt by Armani give **Mira Sorvino** the glamorous look she needed to accept her Best Supporting Actress Oscar for *Mighty Aphrodite*.

MISS AMERICA

The slinky **Vanessa Williams** shows off her Versace gown while singing "Colors of the Wind" from *Pocahontas* on the Academy Awards stage. The sleek metallic mesh gown melds an old-world silhouette with modern fabric technology.

FULL SPEED AHEAD

A strapless satin chocolate-colored Calvin Klein and a thick choker chock full of diamonds make **Sandra Bullock** smile as she strides into the show.

INDEPENDENTS' DAY 1997

Indie films took over the Oscars this year, to the delight of lesser-known stars who finally got their chance to shine. But the big names still stalked the red carpet—both the well-established stars and the mainstream designers they wore.

69TH
ACADEMY AWARDS
March 24, 1997
Shrine Auditorium
Los Angeles
HOST: BILLY CRYSTAL

STAR GAZING
Celine Dion's twinkling Chanel comet necklace, complete with a silvery tail wrapping around her golden vocal chords, was worth nearly half a million dollars.

MAJESTIC IN MAGENTA
Jim Carrey and wife **Lauren Holly** looked like a well-matched pair—she wears a lavender gown strewn with purple flowers, and he sports a purple tuxedo shirt. But their colorful union was short-lived—they divorced a few months later.

AND THE OSCAR® GOES TO...

Best Picture:
The English Patient

Best Director:
Anthony Minghella,
The English Patient

Best Actress:
Frances McDormand,
Fargo

Best Actor:
Geoffrey Rush,
Shine

Best Supporting Actress:
Juliette Binoche,
The English Patient

Best Supporting Actor:
Cuba Gooding Jr.,
Jerry Maguire

1997

Juliette Binoche arrives at the awards in a creamy velvet gown by Sophie Sitbon with a portrait neckline —in a rich shade of *chocolat*.

ENGLAND'S OWN

A black-and-brown silk gown by Christian Lacroix gives British actress **Kristin Scott Thomas**—like her fellow European, Juliette Binoche— a regal glow.

GETTIN' JIGGY WITH IT

Versace designed the matching outfits on **Will** and **Jada Pinkett Smith**. Jada's sparkling green two-piece showed a little skin, and matched the colorful collar peeking out of Will's tuxedo jacket.

KIDDING AROUND

Nicole Kidman (with **Tom Cruise**) cruised the red carpet in a stunning, Asian-inspired chartreuse gown by Christian Dior.

TRUE ROMANCE

Cameron Diaz's two-piece ensemble (admired by **Matt Dillon**) was designed by Stella McCartney for Chloe. The soft, muted colors of the floor-length skirt and full sleeves of the blouse added a little romance to the frenetically glamorous event.

1998 KINGS OF THE WORLD

There were plenty of winners on the red carpet on the night *Titanic* claimed Best Picture. Minimalism had caught on as the way to dress for the awards, and with the new dress code firmly entrenched, the stars were once again having fun with their Oscar-night ensembles.

70TH
ACADEMY AWARDS
March 23, 1998
Shrine Auditorium
Los Angeles
HOST: BILLY CRYSTAL

AND THE OSCAR® GOES TO...

Best Picture:
Titanic

Best Director:
James Cameron,
Titanic

Best Actress:
Helen Hunt,
As Good as It Gets

Best Actor:
Jack Nicholson,
As Good As It Gets

Best Supporting Actress:
Kim Basinger,
L.A. Confidential

Best Supporting Actor:
Robin Williams,
Good Will Hunting

FRESH CATCH
Cher—in yet another Bob Mackie creation—looks like a captured mermaid in this beaded, netted gown with matching hat. With her is her son **Elijah**.

FRESH AS A DAISY
Drew Barrymore dressed up her basic black backless gown by putting fresh daisies in her hair.

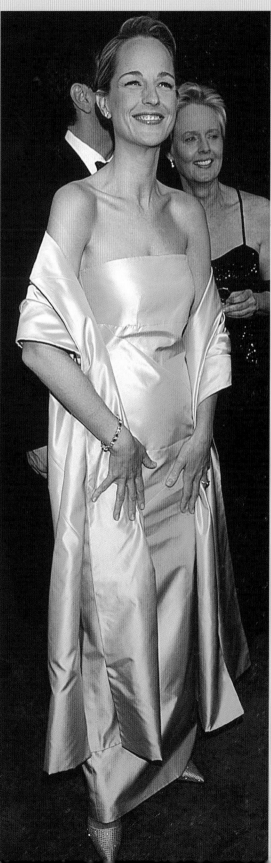

ICE QUEEN

Helen Hunt looks frozen in time in this glamorous ice-blue column gown by Gucci. The satin gown came with a matching wrap to help warm her up.

1998

GOTH GIRL

After **Madonna** wore this gothic black satin coatdress by Oliver Theyskens to the Academy Awards, everybody wanted to celebrate the young Belgian designer.

1998

L.A. CONFIDENTIAL

Kim Basinger proudly displays the Oscar she won for her Best Supporting Actress role in *L.A. Confidential*. She looks every inch the deserving winner in a pistachio-green silk cowl-necked gown by Escada.

HEADLINE MAKER

Sharon Stone paired a men's white button-down shirt—she claimed it belonged to her husband—with a floor-length satin Vera Wang skirt to create one of the most talked about Oscar outfits of the 90s.

GOOD WILL AMBASSADOR

Minnie Driver navigated the red carpet in a fire-engine red Randolph Duke with a slightly trailing train—a detail that would become increasingly popular at future shows. She carries a faux fur wrap that was dyed to match the gown.

LIFE IS BEAUTIFUL 1999

As the decade came to a close, the excitement and hoopla surrounding who would wear what on Oscar night showed no signs of letting up. There was no denying it—what happened outside the auditorium on the red carpet was as much a part of the show as the ceremony that took place inside. The nation's obsession with Oscar-night fashion would only increase as the country entered the new millennium.

71ST
ACADEMY AWARDS
March 21, 1999
Dorothy Chandler Pavilion
Los Angeles
HOST:
WHOOPI GOLDBERG

AND THE OSCAR® GOES TO...

Best Picture:
Shakespeare in Love

Best Director:
Steven Spielberg,
Saving Private Ryan

Best Actress:
Gwyneth Paltrow,
Shakespeare in Love

Best Actor:
Roberto Benigni,
Life Is Beautiful

Best Supporting Actress:
Judi Dench,
Shakespeare in Love

Best Supporting Actor:
James Coburn,
Affliction

HEAD TURNER
Catherine Zeta-Jones wears a strapless red Versace in one of the most popular new silhouettes—floor-length, relatively straight, and displaying a slight train.

LEGENDARY LOOKER
The timelessly chic **Sophia Loren** approaches the podium to announce Best Foreign Language Film in a simply cut black gown by Giorgio Armani with a mesh inset over the décolletage.

1999

PRETTY IN PINK

Gwyneth Paltrow's pink Ralph Lauren seemed to swim around her lithe frame and project sweetness and light. But the $160,000 worth of diamonds around her neck reminded the crowds she was a Hollywood heavyweight.

BRONX ROYALTY

Jennifer Lopez's beaded Badgley Mischka, with its fitted, beaded bodice and full skirt, spins old-fashioned glamour with a modern twist at the end of the century.

LIGHTS OFF

For her first Oscar appearance, **Renee Zellweger** chose a mauve L'Wren Scott gown trimmed with gold that looked more like a lampshade than a star-making gown.

WORTH HER WEIGHT IN PLATINUM

Uma Thurman looks like a modern-day Cleopatra in this two-piece gown from Chanel in platinum, complete with bracelets on either bicep.

WOMAN OVERBOARD

Celine Dion made a titanic mistake when she turned this tux around. Nothing could save this sinking outfit—the rakish hat and cocky shades just added to the tragedy.

GARISH GOWNS

Sometimes the stars just get it wrong—completely wrong. We're not sure whether they're trying to draw attention to themselves with their shockingly bad taste or are just the recipients of some really bad advice from their stylists. (Or perhaps the lack of a stylist altogether is the problem.) In any case, every now and then, even the most tasteful of celebrities puts on an outfit that you makes you wonder if they got their dates confused and thought they were going to a Halloween party. Here's a tour of some of the worst outfits ever to disgrace Oscar's red carpet.

A LOST BETTE
We hate to take the wind from beneath her wings, but couldn't **Bette Midler** have come up with something other than this pea-green cellophane dress?

DRACULA MEETS MOHAWK
Sure, **Cher** is an easy target, but come on … this "gown" has neither aged well nor revealed itself as fashion ahead of its time. (At least not in this century.) Yes, Cher's navel is worthy of gazing at, but did she really need to go to all that trouble to give us a peek?

ONE-ARMED BANDIT
Kim Basinger's 1990 outfit landed her on Mr. Blackwell's worst-dressed list. The nemesis of all celebrities, Blackwell is a self-appointed fashion critic who makes up annual best- and worst-dressed lists of public figures. Basinger's one-gloved, half-jacketed, puffed-out gown with obscure gold lettering on the sleeve makes her look as if she only got half-dressed for the biggest night in Hollywood.

168

1969

NIGHTMARE PAJAMAS

She may have won the Oscar, but **Barbra Streisand** didn't receive many fashion kudos for this over-the-top outfit. The Arnold Scaasi pajamas were strewn with giant translucent sequins and topped off with an incongruous Peter Pan collar with a black bow. Streisand's extra-long fingernails and bi-level bob ensured that this outfit would go down in Oscar history as one of the strangest.

1989

PLEASE DEMI, NO MOORE!

The 80s did very bad things to fashion. Witness this gaudy ensemble, donned by **Demi Moore** in 1989: the bicycle shorts are bad enough, but trying to hide them under that glittering orange brocade bustle is just ugly overkill. With her is **Bruce Willis**.

1991

HE GIVES FASHION A BAD NAME

In a crushed velvet fuchsia suit with a sequined black vest underneath, **Jon Bon Jovi** looks ready to run away and join the circus. Wife Dorothea doesn't fare much better in a purple and blue sequined gown with jagged sleeves. These two are living without a prayer of ever making anyone's best-dressed list.

1993

WOE IS WHOOPI

What was **Whoopi Goldberg** thinking when she wore this whopper of a gown? The purple, gold and lime-green gown was wildly, woefully, weirdly … well, ugly. We hope the funny lady was just joking when she picked it out.

2000s

A RETURN TO ELEGANCE

The understated, refined 90s set just the right tone for the onset of the new millennium, and the first few years of the 2000s confirmed that elegance had indeed returned to the red carpet. The stars wound their way down fashion's most watched catwalk in stylish ensembles put together by themselves, their stylists and the designers who clamored to dress them. Fashion had become inextricably linked with Oscar night, and celebrities (and celebrity watchers) reaped the rewards. Faddish gowns became a thing of the past as elegant, timeless creations returned to prominence. In an era when the awards show had become almost insufferably long, style-watching was a necessary diversion, and one that few can deny is now one of the greatest appeals of the Oscars. Since fashion tends to go in cycles, it's hard to predict how long the new trend for elegant sophistication will hold sway. But one thing's for sure: glamorous, attention-getting gowns will always be in style, especially on Oscar night.

FASHION ON FILM

Moulin Rouge (2001)

This kaleidoscopic dreamscape of a film sparked a brief craze for corsets and tulle skirts, inspired by Nicole Kidman's turn as a can-can girl in 1890s bohemian Paris. The dazzling array of costumes she wore as a dying strumpet who finds love in the twilight of her life spawned a desire among women for vibrant, devil-may-care outfits full of color and attitude.

The Matrix: Reloaded (2003)

The vinyl and latex, faux alligator prints and frameless, bug-eyed sunglasses—all in black—that shrouded the stars of The Matrix *was street fashion amped up, then writ large on the big screen. The sci-fi look of the future was reloaded and filtered back to the masses through knockoffs on city streets everywhere.*

DESIGNERS TO THE STARS: 2000s

NARCISO RODRIGUEZ (1961–)

Fashion's Newest Darling

Narciso Rodriguez shot to fame after designing the wedding gown for Carolyn Bessette's marriage to John F. Kennedy Jr. in 1996. His sleek designs are cut close to the body out of the highest-quality materials, and lend a sexy swagger to their wearers. He has dressed Clare Danes and Salma Hayek, among other actresses.

VERA WANG (1949 –)

From the Wedding Aisle to the Red Carpet

Vera Wang started out designing bridal wear, but soon fans of her work were clamoring for clothes they could wear on occasions other than their wedding days. Her gowns are both romantic and glamorous, hip and old-fashioned, and (not surprisingly) often feature the kind of detailing usually reserved for wedding gowns. Holly Hunter, Sharon Stone and Charlize Theron have all been known to wear the designer's creations.

CAROLINA HERRERA (1939 –)

Late to the Party

Venezuelan-born Carolina Herrera has made her name designing elegant, timeless clothes for the modern woman. Though she came to her career late (at the age of 40) and was initially dismissed as a "society" designer, Herrera has since proven her mettle, and she endures as one of today's most popular designers. Her A-list celebrity clientele has included the likes of Jacqueline Onassis and Renée Zellweger.

2000 THE WAITING GAME

The biggest story of this year's Oscar ceremony was not who was wearing what, but who had stolen all the Oscars? Fifty-five of them mysteriously disappeared, although all but three were recovered before the big night. Luckily, the stars' outfits didn't go missing, and everyone arrived in their finest duds. It was a good thing, too—viewers at home needed something to look at as the longest ceremony yet droned on for a record 4 hours and 3 minutes.

72ND
ACADEMY AWARDS
March 26, 2000
Shrine Auditorium
Los Angeles
HOST: BILLY CRYSTAL

AND THE OSCAR® GOES TO...

Best Picture:
American Beauty

Best Director:
Sam Mendes,
American Beauty

Best Actress:
Hilary Swank,
Boys Don't Cry

Best Actor:
Kevin Spacey,
American Beauty

Best Supporting Actress:
Angelina Jolie,
Girl, Interrupted

Best Supporting Actor:
Michael Caine,
The Cider House Rules

CHARLIE'S ANGEL

Lucy Liu glowed in a custom-made Versace with sunset-colored sequins fanning out from her hip in glittering sunrays, proving that this angel knows how to shine on the red carpet.

SWANKY STYLE

Hilary Swank (with husband **Chad Lowe**) is luminous in this strapless ball gown that glows with a bronzy patina. Also glowing are the $250,000 worth of Asprey & Garrard diamonds encircling Swank's neck.

VAMPING IT UP IN VIOLET

Ashley Judd's simple yet stunning Valentino is gathered at the waist and seems to float around the bodice. She wears a matching wrap and carries a lavender beaded evening clutch.

2000

HIGH-ROLLING GIRL

Heather Graham traded in her *Boogie Nights* roller-skates for a pearl-encrusted, flesh-toned gown topped with a Fred Leighton necklace featuring 50 carats of diamond briolettes. She arrives on the red carpet with actor **Ed Burns**.

GENIUS, REVISITED

Indie film star **Chloe Sevigny** puts a young spin on a classic Yves Saint Laurent gown. The elegant backless black wrap dress with a plunging neckline and belted waist showed everyone she was no longer a kid. She holds hands with filmmaker **Harmony Korine**.

TRAFFIC JAM *2001*

There was a glut of glamour on the red carpet this year. The stars were showing their true colors in a dazzling array of gorgeous gowns in a rainbow of colors and styles, with a few surprises thrown into the mix. But one variable held constant—the gowns were well-designed and almost always flattered their wearers.

73RD
ACADEMY AWARDS
March 25, 2001
Shrine Auditorium
Los Angeles
HOST: STEVE MARTIN

ROBERTS' ROLE OF A LIFETIME

Who could forget the vintage Valentino **Julia Roberts** wore when she won the Oscar for her starring role in *Erin Brockovich*? The floor-length stunner features a racy white stripe down its front and several more stripes in the back, which fans out into a black tulle train. She walks the red carpet with **Benjamin Bratt**.

AND THE OSCAR® GOES TO...

Best Picture:
Gladiator

Best Director:
Steven Soderbergh,
Traffic

Best Actress:
Julia Roberts,
Erin Brockovich

Best Actor:
Russell Crowe,
Gladiator

Best Supporting Actress:
Marcia Gay Harden,
Pollock

Best Supporting Actor:
Benicio Del Toro,
Traffic

2001

CORAL BEAUTY

Joan Allen stands out from the crowd in a floor-length turtleneck gown by Michael Kors in an eye-popping shade of coral (embellished with real coral beads), proving that actresses don't have to bare cleavage to look stunning—a gorgeous color and cut can also do the trick.

SWAN SONG

Icelandic pop star **Björk** wears what in the annals of Oscar fashion history has come to be known as the "swan dress." Designed by her fellow Icelandic friend Marjan Pejoski, the daring outfit drew raves from some and critical clucking from the less open-minded.

THE TWO COCOS

Actress **Coco Lee** wears another Coco, that of the house of Chanel. The brightly colored sequined stripes and black chiffon inlays along the gown's sides made for an electric Oscar-night look.

STEELY BEAUTY

A sheerly wrapped **Jennifer Lopez** shows off Chanel in a steel-gray see-through top coupled with a sweeping silvery satin skirt. Lopez smartly lets the gown take center stage and downplays her accessories with just a diamond cuff bracelet and long, dangling earrings.

2002 A BEAUTIFUL NIGHT

74TH
ACADEMY AWARDS
March 24, 2002
Kodak Theater
Hollywood
HOST:
WHOOPI GOLDBERG

Oscar history was made this year, as Halle Berry became the first black actress ever to win the Best Actress Oscar. Her choice of gown on the historic night was worthy of the attention the actress received—the beautiful, deep red embroidered Elie Saab creation comes in first place in some polls of fans' favorite Oscar dresses of all time. (See *Oscar's Most Beautiful Gowns*, p. 132, for photo and information).

AND THE OSCAR® GOES TO...

Best Picture:
A Beautiful Mind

Best Director:
Ron Howard,
A Beautiful Mind

Best Actress:
Halle Berry,
Monster's Ball

Best Actor:
Denzel Washington,
Training Day

Best Supporting Actress:
Jennifer Connelly,
A Beautiful Mind

Best Supporting Actor:
Jim Broadbent,
Iris

MAKING WAVES

Kate Winslet's crimson Ben de Lisi gown is embellished with a silk-rose-garland shoulder strap that recalls the style of Spanish flamenco dancers.

IN THE FLESH

The flamenco theme shows up again in **Jennifer Connolly's** strapless nude Balenciaga gown, which featured tattered tiers of fabric on the skirt and a matching long chiffon scarf.

REESE'S PIECE

This beaded Valentino is so beautiful it should be illegal. The delicate lace, cap sleeves and elaborate beading put **Reese Witherspoon** at the top of the fashion heap.

179

2002

SPRING FLING

A column of soft-pink chiffon ruffles encircles **Nicole Kidman** (with sister **Antonia Kidman-Hawley**) as she arrives on the red carpet. Along with the Chanel gown, Kidman wears a $4 million, 241-carat Bulgari diamond necklace she helped design.

ON THE MONEY

In Carolina Herrera's midnight blue strapless gown with a trailing beaded-hem train, **Renée Zellweger** shows off her maturing fashion instincts.

THE ANNIVERSARY PARTY 2003

Celebrating 75 years, the Oscar's diamond anniversary wasn't nearly as flashy as its name suggests. With a war being waged in Iraq, the red-carpet extravaganza was scaled back, and the stars respectfully opted to minimize the usual dazzle of Oscar night jewels in favor of more subdued looks. But that didn't stop the celebrities from taking center stage in a bevy of gorgeous gowns. If anything, the somber mood of the nation may have helped temper the stars' otherwise flamboyant tastes, resulting in a parade of gorgeous dresses that were more beautiful in their subtleties than anything of the years immediately prior. As one fashion commentator put it, "style and elegance have come full circle."

75TH
ACADEMY AWARDS
March 23, 2003
Kodak Theater
Hollywood
HOST: STEVE MARTIN

GOLDIE'S GIRL
Kate Hudson (daughter of **Goldie Hawn**) shines in a dazzling gold beaded lace Versace gown that matches her golden blonde hair.

AND THE OSCAR® GOES TO...

Best Picture:
Chicago

Best Director:
Roman Polanski,
The Pianist

Best Actress:
Nicole Kidman,
The Hours

Best Actor:
Adrien Brody,
The Pianist

Best Supporting Actress:
Catherine Zeta-Jones,
Chicago

Best Supporting Actor:
Chris Cooper,
Adaptation

QUEEN OF THE NIGHT
Queen Latifah strikes a regal pose in a smoky blue gown by Bradley Bayou for Halston. Her bejeweled clutch, festooned with $2.9 million in diamonds, was fit for royalty.

WELL RED

For the second year in a row, **Renée Zellweger** chose a Carolina Herrera gown, this time in a rich crimson that showed up the red carpet itself. The delicately beaded bodice glittered so much that Zellweger downplayed the rest of the ensemble with nothing but a giant ruby ring on her left hand—and ruby red lips.

WEARING OSCAR AT THE OSCARS

Diane Lane's Oscar de la Renta gown was originally two—the draped top is from one gown, and the feathery beige bottom was cut from another. Together, they add up to one gorgeous gown.

GOLDEN EYE

Halle Berry proves once again that she has the style to match her beauty. Wearing an Elie Saab gown for the second year in a row, Berry's gleaming, one-shouldered gown sparkles almost as much as she does.

ANGEL IN BLACK

Her hair looks a little bit bedraggled, but in this pleated black chiffon Prada gown with sequined belt, **Cameron Diaz** is a knockout.

SPOTLIGHT
on Gowns: EARLY 2000s

NICOLE GETS RECAST AS A GREEK GODDESS

Draped in **JEAN PAUL GAULTIER**, Nicole Kidman evoked the image of a Greek goddess, though her gown was thoroughly modern. Made of black silk jersey, the dress's complex lines created visual intrigue without distracting from the silhouette of Nicole's statuesque frame. Her tightly pulled-back hair and minimal jewelry echoed the understated look of many of the stars in 2003, and helped her make a stunning style statement.

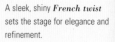

A sleek, shiny *French twist* sets the stage for elegance and refinement.

Diamond chandelier earrings by Fred Leighton add sparkle and subdued drama.

Expertly draped jersey gathers in all the right places, adding a serious dose of sex appeal.

The *asymmetrical neckline* is made up of three pieces of fabric wrapped strategically around the shoulder and neck—an innovative and offbeat take one of the year's top trends.

As she walks, the heavier folds of the material swish away, exposing the *sheer panel at the base of the gown* and giving us a glimpse of Nicole's legs.

Strappy leather sandals—custom made for Nicole by Pierre Hardy—echo the crisscross look of the dress's neckline.

CHARLIZE THERON
CHARLIZE'S TANGERINE DREAM

Charlize Theron's backless **VERA WANG** gown turned heads with its fresh take on the glamour-girl look. The dress borrowed details from nearly every decade and mixed them together in an eye-popping shade that perked up everybody's fashion senses.

Charlize's *short, precisely curled hair* recalled 1920s flapper styles.

A *halter-neck top* frames a long, swan-like neck, sans jewelry.

In a nod to the brooches often used to cinch fabric in the 30s, Charlize added two *Fred Leighton diamond clips* to the gown

The *cut and fabric* allow the gown to skim Charlize's figure—and show it off—without being excessively tight. The gown is cut dangerously low in back and gathered at the posterior.

A frothy *train of silk* follows Charlize as she walks and adds motion to the gown.

JULIANNE MOORE's
STRIKING COLOR CHOICE MAKES A HUE STATEMENT

The rich, emerald color of Julianne Moore's strapless chiffon gown, by **YVES SAINT LAURENT RIVE GAUCHE**, contrasts beautifully with her naturally red hair. Wearing a dress this saturated in color is a bold move, since selecting the wrong color can ruin the whole look, but Julianne pulls it off splendidly. Like Nicole, she left her neckline bare, and for jewelry selected only a pair of drop earrings.

A refined *French twist*, a classic Oscar do, makes Julianne's red hair gleam, a glorious contrast to the color of the gown.

Dangling Boucheron emerald and diamond earrings set in black gold are the only accessories this dazzling dress needs.

The color says it all—this deep, rich emerald hue makes a fashion statement all on its own.

Ruffles cascading down the front of the gown enliven its shape and add movement.

The gown's *frothy fabric and asymmetrical hemline* add sass to Julianne's look as she slinks down the red carpet.

Shoes with ankle straps are always sexy, but wrapped around Julianne's dainty ankles, these matching heels add *va-va-voom* to an elegant getup.

INDEX

BIBLIOGRAPHY

E! Online: www.eonline.com
Fox, Patty. Star Style at the Academy Awards: A Century of Glamour. Santa Monica: Angel City Press, 2000.
Kinn, Gail, and Jim Piazza. The Academy Awards: The Complete History of Oscar. New York: Black Dog & Leventhal, 2002.
Peacock, John. The Fashion Sourcebooks, 7 vols. London: Thames & Hudson, 1997-98.
People Magazine, eds. Oscar Style: 75 Years of Hollywood Glitter and Glamour. New York: Time, Inc., 2003.
Seeling, Charlotte. Fashion: The Century of the Designer. Cologne: Könemann, 2000.

PHOTOGRAPHY CREDITS

Photofest
pp. 6 (left, right), 7 (right) 8, 9, 10 (left, right), 14, 15 (top left, bottom left), 16, 17, 18, 19, 22, 23 (left, right), 24, 26, 27 (center, bottom left, top right), 28, 29 (top left, bottom left), 30 (right) 31 (center, right), 34, 35 (left, right), 36, 38 (top right, bottom right), 39 (left, right), 40 (bottom left, right), 41 (center right), 44 (top left, bottom left), 45, 46 (left), 47 (left, center, right), 48 (right), 49 (left), 50, 52 (left, bottom), 53 (left), 55 (top right), 56 (top right), 58, 59 (bottom left, top left), 60 (left), 61 (top right), 62 (bottom left), 63 (top left, bottom), 64 (top left, top right), 65 (top right, bottom), 68 (top left), 69 (bottom right), 70 (top right, bottom right), 71 (bottom right), 75 (bottom left, top right), 76 (right), 78 (bottom left, right), 81 (left), 82 (bottom right), 84 (bottom right), 86 (top left), 89 (right), 90 (top right, bottom right), 91 (top right), 96 (bottom right), 100, 101 (bottom left, top left), 102 (right), 114 (left), 120 (left), 132 (left), 134, 135 (top left, bottom left), 169 (top left), 170, 171 (top left, bottom left).

Globe Photos, Inc.
Phil Roach/Globe Photos, Inc.: pp. 77 (bottom left), 81 (bottom, right), 84 (top left), 85 (bottom right), 86 (right), 87 (top left), 90 (bottom left), 91 (bottom left), 92 (top left), 93 (top left, bottom left), 95 (top right), 97 (top left, bottom left, bottom right), 99 (bottom left), 102 (right), 103 (right), 104 (left, right), 105 (right), 106 (left, top right, bottom right), 107 (left), 108 (left, right), 109 (left, top right, bottom right), 110 (left, right), 113 (left), 116 (right), 117 (bottom left), 125 (bottom right), 129 (left, right), 130 (right), 131 (top right), 141 (right), 142, 169 (top right). Nate Cutler/Globe Photos, Inc.: pp. 77 (top left), 78 (top left), 79 (top right, bottom right), 83 (top left, top right, bottom right), 90 (top left), 91 (top right, bottom right), 92 (right), 93 (top right, bottom right), 94 (top right, bottom), 95 (bottom left, bottom right), 97 (top right), 99 (top right), 103 (top left, bottom right), 118. James Colburn/Globe Photos, Inc.: pp. 111 (right), 114 (right), 121 (left, bottom right), 122 (left), 123 (bottom), 124 (right), 125 (right), 128 (center), 168 (right). Ralph Dominguez/Globe Photos, Inc.: pp. 115 (left, top right, bottom right), 124 (left), 128 (left, right), 131 (left), 137 (right), 138, 139 (left). Michael Ferguson/Globe Photos, Inc.: pp. 143 (left, right), 147 (right), 149 (left). Tammie Arroyo/Globe Photos, Inc.: p. 166 (left). Rose Hartman/Globe Photos, Inc.: p. 135 (center right, bottom right). Roger Karnbad/Globe Photos, Inc.: pp. 131 (bottom right), 136. Sonia Moskowitz/Globe Photos, Inc.: p. 135 (top right). Bob Noble/Globe Photos, Inc.: p. 94 (left). Ned Redway/Globe Photos, Inc.: p. 153 (right). Andrea Renault/Globe Photos, Inc.: p. 151 (bottom). Lisa Rose/Globe Photos, Inc.: p. 165 (left). Joyce Silverstein/Globe Photos, Inc.: p. 167 (center). Globe Photos, Inc.: pp. 13, 83 (bottom left), 85 (top left), 87 (bottom left), 111 (left), 112 (bottom left, right), 113 (right), 116 (left), 119 (left), 144 (left, right), 149 (center), 151 (left), 164 (right), 168 (left).

Associated Press
pp. 11 (left, right), 15 (center right, bottom right), 20, 27 (top left, bottom right), 30 (left), 31 (left), 32 (left, right), 33, 37, 40 (top left), 41 (top right), 44 (right), 48 (left), 49 (center, right), 51, 52 (top right), 53 (top right, bottom right), 54 (left, right), 55 (top left, bottom), 56 (center right, bottom left, center left), 57 (top right, center right, bottom left), 59 (top right), 61 (bottom), 62 (top), 63 (top right), 64 (bottom), 65 (top left), 68 (bottom), 70 (top left), 71 (left, top right), 72 (right), 76 (left), 80 (left, right), 82 (left, top right), 84 (top right), 86 (bottom left), 89 (left), 92 (bottom), 95 (top left), 96 (top left, right), 99 (top left, bottom right), 101 (bottom right), 105 (left), 112 (right), 117 (top), 120 (right), 121 (top), 123 (top), 126 (top, bottom), 127 (top, bottom), 130 (left), 132 (center left, center right), 133 (left, center left, center right), 137 (left), 139 (right), 140 (top), 141 (left), 145 (left, right), 147 (top left, bottom left), 148 (left, right), 150 (center left, bottom left, right), 152 (center, right), 156 (left, right), 157 (left), 158 (right), 161 (left), 162 (left), 164 (left, center), 165 (right), 167 (right), 168 (center), 171 (top right, center right, bottom right), 172, 173 (left, right), 174 (left, right), 175, 176 (right), 177 (right), 178, 179 (left, right), 180 (left, right), 181 (left, right), 182 (left, right), 183 (left, right), 184 (left), 185 (left).

Hulton Archive/Getty Images
Hulton Archive/Getty Images: pp. 12 (right), 15 (top right), 21, 29 (center right, bottom right), 43 (center right, bottom right), 57 (top left), 59 (bottom right), 60 (right), 61 (right), 69 (top right), 72 (left), 75 (bottom right), 77 (right), 79 (left), 85 (left), 101 (top right), 117 (left). Bill Brandt/Getty Images: p. 29 (top right). Ron Case/Getty Images: p. 75 (center right). Frank Edwards/Getty Images: p. 87 (bottom right). Darlene Hammond/Getty Images: 61 (top left). Gene Lester/Getty Images: p.12 (left), 69 (right). John Minihan/Getty Images: p. 59 (center right). Robert Scott/Getty Images: p. 119 (right).

Corbis
© Bettmann/CORBIS: pp. 7 (left), 38 (left), 42, 43 (bottom left, top left), 46 (right), 62 (bottom right), 66, 67 (left, right), 70 (bottom left), 73 (bottom right, bottom left), 74, 75 (top left), 88, 117 (left). © Julio Donoso/CORBIS SYGMA: 101 (center right). © Los Angeles Daily News/Sprague David/CORBIS SYGMA: 41 (left). © Sophie Bassouls/CORBIS SYGMA: 43 (top right).

picturedesk.com/The Kobal Collection: p. 25

WireImage.com: Steve Granitz/WireImage.com: p. 153 (bottom left), 155 (center), 157 (top right), 158 (left, bottom), 167 (left), 176 (left), 177 (left), 184 (center). Dan MacMedan/WireImage.com: p. 185 (right). Jeffrey Mayer/WireImage.com: p. 154 (right), 159 (right), 160 (right). Kevin Mazur/WireImage.com: pp. 140 (bottom), 146 (left, center, right), 151 (left), 152 (left), 153 (top left), 155 (left), 157 (bottom right), 159 (left), 160 (left, center), 161 (right), 162 (right), 163 (left, right), 166 (right), 169 (bottom right, bottom left), 185 (center).

Cover photographs are reprinted by permission of The Associated Press, except for Audrey Hepburn ("C"), Loretta Young (first "A"), Eva Marie Saint ("R") and Grace Kelly ("H"), by permission of Photofest.

Reeve Chace has reported on fashion and beauty for InStyle magazine, the Providence Journal Bulletin and AOL's DigitalCity, among other print and Web publications. She is a writer and editor for books and magazines, and was the fashion consultant for The Academy Awards: The Complete History of Oscar. She lives in New York City.